HOW TO ...
identify and overcome handwriting difficulties

Lois M. Addy

Acknowledgements

Thank you to the children and young people who I have had the privilege to support over the past 30+ years in overcoming their handwriting difficulties, for what you have taught me in your struggles to create legible script. This has led me to seek effective interventions which can alleviate some of your distress.

Thank you also to the NYCC specialist ATAs who have become experts in addressing children's handwriting difficulties. They include Jill Ash, Wendy Walker, Jacky Blakeley, Helen Robson, Liz Ramsay, Lisa Maddison, Judy Davey, Glenda Pearce and Celia Kennedy.

How to identify and overcome handwriting difficulties

ISBN: 978-1-85503-602-4

© Lois M. Addy 2016

Illustrations by Robin Lawrie (pp. 5, 10, 11, 12, 13, 14, 15, 16, 17, 18, 20, 27, 43b, 44, 49, 55, 63, 65, 96, 97, 99, 100, 104), Ray & Corinne Burrows/Beehive Illustration (pp. 21, 25, 32, 33, 35, 36, 37, 38), Mike Phillips/Beehive Illustration (pp. 71, 72), James Alexander (pp. 43a, 43c, 46, 47)

This edition published 2016
10 9 8 7 6 5 4 3 2

Printed in the UK by Page Bros (Norwich) Ltd
Designed and typeset by Andy Wilson for Green Desert Ltd

LDA, 2 Gregory Street, Hyde, Cheshire, SK14 4HR

www.ldalearning.com

The right of Lois Addy to be identified as the author of this work has been asserted in accordance with Sections 77 and 78 of the Copyright, Designs and Patents Act 1988.

All rights reserved. This book contains materials which may be reproduced by photocopier or other means for use by the purchaser. The permission is granted on the understanding that these copies will be used within the educational establishment of the purchaser. The book and all its contents remain copyright. Copies may be made without reference to the publisher or the licensing scheme for the making of photocopies operated by the Publishers Licensing Society.

CONTENTS

	Preface	v
1	Introduction	1
2	Ergonomic and biomechanical aspects of handwriting	9
3	Handedness and pen(cil) grip	23
4	A process-orientated approach to handwriting	39
5	A task-specific approach to handwriting	53
6	When to use technology: a compensatory approach to handwriting	59
7	Assessment and intervention	67
8	Conclusion	94
	Appendix A: Pelvic girdle stability activities	96
	Appendix B: Shoulder girdle stability activities	100
	Appendix C: In-hand manipulation activities	103
	References	105

PREFACE

I and my like-minded teacher colleagues questioned the value of handwriting instruction in an already overcrowded language arts curriculum and particularly in an increasingly technologically-orientated world. In short, I believed what many teachers believed: that handwriting instruction could be neglected without penalising students. I was wrong!

Reutzel, 2015

Handwriting is 'language by hand'. It remains the most effective form of written communication and is used extensively in childhood and less frequently in adulthood. We record our knowledge and our thoughts and emotions; we write lists, sign cards, take notes, and pen stories. However, handwriting is a complex skill requiring perception, motor co-ordination, cognition and linguistic processing. It requires careful instruction and opportunities to practise, especially during the early years. Unfortunately, between 10–30% of children and young people struggle to produce clear, comprehensible script. This has a profound effect on their self-confidence, educational achievement, and subsequent enjoyment of literacy per se (Medwell & Wray, 2007; Overelde & Hustijn, 2011).

As an occupational therapist and educator, I have witnessed many children and young people struggling to control pencil and paper to produce legible writing at a speed that is acceptable to the educational task in hand, and have seen their frustration when they see the mismatch between their effort and the end product. Given that approximately 50% of pupils' time in primary school involves writing-related tasks, it is no surprise that their self-esteem can quickly plummet and we see a reluctance to write; this being especially true of boys (Dennis & Swinth, 2001; Rosenblum et al., 2004; Stainthorp & Rauf, 2009). I often reflect on whether I would continue in a role where 50% of my tasks were effortful and exhausting, and the end product mediocre!

Writing consists of **transcription** and **composition**. Effective transcription requires intricate motor dexterity to manipulate the writing tool with appropriate pressure and fluent movement; an accurate appreciation of form constancy, figure-ground discrimination and spatial planning to ensure its legibility; and an understanding of letter sounds and symbols, and an appreciation of how these connect to create words and subsequent sentences. Composition involves the generation of ideas, sentence construction, spelling, grammar, punctuation and emphasis. Teachers are experts in the latter, but (due to the complexity of the neurological processes involved) often need support in understanding the reasons why some children struggle with the transcription aspects of handwriting. In one study involving 188 teachers across 10 primary schools in London and South East England,

45% of the teachers reported that struggling writers were a problem for them (Dockrell et al., 2016). Handwriting is not typically addressed in initial teacher training, so postgraduate training is required. The availability of this can be sporadic and therefore inconsistencies can arise in the support these children are offered.

After observing those who struggle to write, I have devoted considerable time to evaluating why some children seem to be able to master this skill with ease while others find it so problematic. This has led me to analyse ergonomic constraints such as classroom furniture (e.g. table height, seating position, writing tools) and biomechanical factors such as individual posture and pencil grip, and the components involved in mastering this complex skill. This is a continuing journey which has so far spanned 34 years (and which, undoubtedly, will never reach a given destination). Over this time I have seen some curious changes in writing habits, with pencil grips that were previously classed as 'abnormal' or 'inefficient' becoming commonplace; perhaps reflecting the evolutionary use of the thumb due to texting and gaming. I have seen the introduction of alternative methods of writing enabling those who have so much to express record their thoughts in an intelligible manner. At the same time, I have seen a growing hesitancy from teachers as they consider the dilemma as to whether to spend their time investing in technology or practising handwriting.

This challenge to handwriting comes from a flood of technology which provides an alternative to traditional handwriting, which is being embraced by children and adults alike. Some countries have overtly stated that they are disposing of cursive handwriting tuition in favour of technology. For example, Minna Harmanen from the National Board of Education in Finland issued a statement that 'from 2016, pupils will be taught only print writing and will spend more time learning keyboard skills' (Russell, 2015). These kind of declarations leave many educators wondering whether handwriting is a skill which will ultimately become redundant.

This has been counteracted by a wave of protest from neurologists who are increasingly voracious in highlighting the importance of handwriting to cognition and linguistics, and subsequently reading, especially during a child's formative years. The complex interactions involved in manipulating a pencil, the perceptual appreciation of form and direction in the process of creating letters, and the linguistic processes involved in ascribing a sound to a letter, leading to letter combinations producing words which convey meaning, cannot be replicated by the limited motor effort involved in pressing keys on a keyboard.

The immediacy of written communication has not yet been superseded by technology, although digital advances are bombarding educators with programmes and apps which purport to replace the effort of handwriting, releasing valuable teaching time to focus on the core subjects of maths, English and science. However, whilst technology can provide some opportunities for supporting literacy, it cannot replace the motor planning kinaesthetic processes which form crucial memories fundamental to the handwriting process.

This text supports the arguments of psychologists and neurologists in reiterating the importance of introducing transcription during a child's formative years, and explains its cognitive benefits to future achievements in literacy. It focuses on the various approaches that teachers can adopt to support those who are struggling to produce legible handwriting and the rationale and evidence base for each. Dockrell et al.'s study (2016) identified that teachers felt that they had limited resources to support children who were struggling to write. There may appear to be a disparity between this view and the number of writing programmes which seem to be available on the market. However, the issue for many teachers is *which* resource or intervention to use. Indeed, it is impossible to recommend one programme over another; just as handwriting is a complex process, so is the solution. However, selected programmes have been referred to in this text. This is intended to give teachers the tools and resources with which they can make informed choices and create personalised interventions to address individual needs.

Further programmes, resources and interventions can be sourced through membership of the National Handwriting Association. This provides excellent advice on handwriting resources and publishes regular research which provides the evidence base for selected approaches and interventions, which can help teachers to identify personal solutions to practical problems while enhancing their own knowledge and expertise. As a long-term member, I have benefitted from the national and international guidance this association has provided over many years.

Handwriting may continue to challenge educators and pupils alike, but it is a unique part of our culture and has more utility than it is given credit for. It will continue to provide a creative means of self-expression which reflects individual personality and emotions through words, emphasis, style and presentation. I hope that readers will share this perspective while remaining open to the support that new technology can bring to this educational arena.

Lois M. Addy

> *There's something incredibly powerful about making your mark on paper. It's the moment when an idea leaves your mind and looks back at you for the first time. I've never been able to replicate that experience digitally. It's not unlike Skyping with a close friend vs. having them over for dinner.*
>
> Ryder Carroll

CHAPTER 1
Introduction

Why write?

In this rapidly progressing technological age in which children and young people are becoming highly proficient in communicating by text, type and other virtual modalities, do we still need to learn to write by hand? This question is particularly important at a time when schools appear to be de-emphasising the art of handwriting.

Finding the answer requires us to examine the *process* of writing, and to carefully consider the developmental attributes connected to language, reading, comprehension, perception, motor planning and action. We must also analyse the evidence that explores the neurological and kinaesthetic processes involved in producing handwriting. This book will later ask whether technology can provide the same benefits.

The process of handwriting

When writing is embedded throughout the curriculum, it promotes the brain's attentive focus to class- and homework, boosts long-term memory, illuminates patterns, gives the brain time for reflection, and when well-guided is a source of conceptual development and stimulus of the brain's highest cognition.
Willis, 2011

Handwriting is a multi-faceted skill. Before putting pen to paper, we need to generate and select ideas; engage in linguistic planning; visualise, order and plan letter forms to create words and sentences; and execute the motor processes to produce culturally-explicit symbols, leading to legible script which considers transcription, spelling and punctuation. The instigation of these components demands considerable neurological effort during a very early stage in child development. In the UK, we expect children to begin to learn to write between 4–5 years of age. In other countries (such as Sweden), this is not introduced until children have had the opportunity to experience and develop the linguistic, kinaesthetic and motor skills which form the foundations of handwriting. The following aspects of neurological development provide the basis from which the compositional aspects of handwriting can emerge.

Motor skills

The fine motor control needed to produce legible handwriting is considerable, and the early development of intricate dexterity is a vital component of the writing process. The **unilateral** (or one-handed) nature of handwriting has the benefit of enhancing specific hemispheres of the brain that relate to motor control, language and literacy. This activity therefore helps to form key connections between areas of the brain that relate to language and literacy. Evidence from magnetic resonance imaging (MRI) brain scans shows that these networks are less evident when word processing than handwriting (Dehaene, 2011).

Although handwriting is a unilateral skill, the non-dominant hand, rather than being passive, 'frames' the movement of the dominant hand and helps to establish the spatial context in which the skilled movements involved in handwriting will take place. The subtle adjustments of the position of the writing paper, together with the movement of the arm and hand across the page, encourage skills which demand the similar integration of both hands like those involved in activities such as fastening and unfastening buttons, opening a can and unscrewing a toothpaste lid (Mangen & Velay, 2010).

The motor learning element of handwriting (which involves good posture, refined manual dexterity and the careful adjustment of pressure through the writing media) provides the **motor memories** required for writing which will ultimately become automatic. This affects the speed of output and endurance to complete the amount of text required, be this for an examination or the composition of a report, letter or story. Research has shown that the ability to produce handwriting at an effective speed can predict everything from a pupil's quality and quantity of written compositions, to their ability to take notes, to the scores they receive in school examinations (Peverly et al., 2014).

Cognition

This involves perceptual understanding arising from the interpretation of sensory input. It also incorporates working and long-term memory, and the mental processes which help us to gain knowledge and ascribe meaning to our experiences. Cognition enables us to think, know, remember, interpret, judge and problem-solve. Therefore, handwriting demands the accurate processing of:

- perception
- memory
- language.

Perception

Handwriting involves many perceptual dimensions, in particular **visual-motor integration** and **visual-spatial planning**. Visual-motor integration (or hand–eye co-ordination) provides a vital link between the hand and the eyes. This enables the writer to clearly observe and co-ordinate the writing process. It helps with visual tracking, which is essential when writing words (which travel horizontally from left to right in English). Visual-spatial planning helps with the organisation of writing on a page and the spaces required between words. The skills obtained through this process also help with the judgement of space during other activities such as locating the players and ball during a game of football; organising numbers in columns during a maths exercise; or manoeuvring around obstacles when, for example, cycling.

Letter formation requires the understanding of shapes and proportions, which involves perception of form (or **form constancy**). The physical experience of producing letters helps individuals to learn about variations in direction, size, connections and shape, and this in turn helps with the development of both locational concepts (e.g. under, on, next to), and also the recognition of other similarly-shaped objects. This helps children start to categorise shapes and lines (e.g. a circle), and vertical and horizontal lines, their sizes and orientations, allowing them to understand the perceptual properties of the letter forms. The process of categorisation stimulates a particular area of the brain known as the **fusiform gyrus**. This becomes particularly active when free-printing, drawing and tracing letters, helping the child to identify and recognise letters (James & Engelhardt, 2012; Alonso, 2015).

Interestingly, the sensory modalities involved in handwriting (i.e. vision, touch and movement) are so intimately entwined that they develop strong neural connections which help children and young people to not only read and write letters in English, but also different languages and symbol and writing systems (Longcamp et al., 2005; James & Gauthier, 2006; Vinter & Chartrel, 2008).

Unfortunately, difficulties in acquiring the visual-motor and visual-spatial aspects of handwriting due to anomalies in perceptual development will influence the writer's ability to appreciate space and form. Writing will become distorted and illegible and this in turn will hinder the fluency and automaticity vital for the expression of ideas. The ability to automatically generate handwriting on paper without having to think increases the speed and volume of output and therefore a lack of automaticity severely restricts the creative writing process (Graham & MacArthur, 2013; Wicki et al., 2014; Dinehart, 2015).

Memory

Cognition requires the interplay of important **executive functions** which help us to organise, plan and complete tasks. These enable us to juggle numerous processes at one time; this is evident when writing. A key aspect of executive functioning is memory, of which there are a variety of types. Handwriting triggers the activation of short- and long-term memory through visual, kinaesthetic and motor recall.

Motor memories are formed from feedback obtained through receptors in the muscles, tendons and joints in the hand, wrist and arm during the act of writing. This feedback is known as **kinaesthesia**, and is essential for hand–eye co-ordination, planning movements, and applying accurate pressure through the pen or pencil. These movements provide a motor memory (or imprint), which is then reinforced by the visual image of the letter. The memory of the letter form is strengthened by repetition and practice, providing long-term letter recognition (Velay & Longcamp, 2012). Contrarily, the motor skills involved in using a keyboard do not require movements which replicate the shape of the letter. The writing action consists of deciding which key to press, and therefore does not provide the combined kinaesthetic and visual memories so necessary during the early years (Longcamp et al., 2005).

Writing with a pencil is typically slower than word processing and this has a positive effect on establishing kinaesthetic memories while providing the writer time to link the letter-sound knowledge to the appropriate letter symbol. This gives the memory a greater opportunity to respond to and store information from the 'inner voice'. This 'inner voice' involves the child internally replaying the letter sound; this encodes the verbal and acoustic information into the memory's storage system (this is technically referred to as the **sub-vocal articulatory rehearsal process**). This process provides positive reinforcement to the working memory, and subsequently results in greater retention of letter sounds and shapes (Chenoweth & Hayes, 2003).

The value of kinaesthetic memory can be appreciated by those with established handwriting. For example, consider the simple task of food shopping. Most shopping lists are handwritten. The list serves as a prompt to remind the buyer what to purchase when going up and down the supermarket aisles. However, once written, the shopper may only occasionally glance at the list to check that all the items have been collected. The reason for this is that the mental energy involved in identifying the items of food required, together with the motor effort involved in writing the list, reinforces the working memory to such an extent that there is little need to revisit the shopping list. Interestingly, typed shopping lists do not have the same effect, meaning that the shopper needs to check the list more regularly throughout their shopping trip.

Similarly, Mueller & Oppenheimer (2014) found that university students who handwrote notes in lectures had a better grasp of the subject over a longer period of time than those who used a laptop to record their notes, surmising that the act of taking notes by hand can activate kinaesthetic memories that contribute to long-term learning (Smoker et al., 2009; Mueller, 2014; Alonso, 2015).

Language

The act of physically producing letters, sounding them out and connecting them to create words reinforces the connections between language and literacy. Brain imaging shows that there is more activity in areas of the brain known to underlie successful reading when children write letters than when they type or trace them. In addition, the physical act of forming letter shapes while sounding them out to create phonetically plausible words can subsequently support future spelling (James & Engelhardt, 2012; Perfetti & Tan, 2013; Maldarelli et al., 2015).

Early attempts at replicating letters to form words provide the linguistic connections which open the doors to imagination, promoting levels of ideation and composition. This is subsequently enhanced by the introduction to punctuation, tone and emphasis. Although the base skills of handwriting may require considerable experimentation and practice to master, they can ultimately enable individuals to unlock ideas and concepts that are not evident in their present environment, or indeed reality (McCarney et al., 2013).

Handwriting provides a gateway to reading. It could be predicted that difficulties in one will relate to the other (Berninger et al., 2008). However, this depends on the nature of the difficulty. For example, children with developmental co-ordination disorder (DCD) can often read very well, but their writing can be illegible due to poor motor co-ordination. In those with dyslexia, it is often the process of sequencing letters to create words that hinders their writing ability, rather than the handwriting process itself (Sumner et al., 2013). The good news is that it is possible to teach both word decoding and handwriting together (Berninger & Richards, 2012). For example, programmes such as *Fun with Phonics: Handwriting* by CBeebies, *Letters and Sounds*, *Sounds-Write* by First Rate Phonics, and *Read Write Inc* by Ruth Minskin show positive improvements in both reading and handwriting legibility.

Word processing

The evidence provides us with an effective argument for the continued teaching of handwriting (especially during the early years), emphasising the importance of kinaesthetic feedback reinforced by the visual image of each letter, supplemented by the letter sounds which are phonetically connected to create words which have meaning for the individual. We need to ask whether other virtual modes of written communication can provide the same benefits.

Evidence shows that it is a fallacy that word processing requires fewer skills than handwriting. Complex spatial planning is needed to negotiate a QWERTY keyboard, the structure of which is at odds with the sequence of the English alphabet. However, the identification of and light pressure on the appropriate keys on a keyboard do not serve to reinforce the shape and form of letters through kinaesthetic experience as the muscles of the hand are not stimulated in the same way that the manipulation of a pencil demands. Information written on a keyboard is produced so rapidly that the input to the kinaesthetic sense is minimal and the subsequent motor and visual memories are therefore more fleeting (Longcamp et al., 2008; James, 2010; Mangen et al., 2010; Alonso, 2015).

Research has indicated that the connecting strokes of cursive (joined-up) handwriting may help to link letters to spelling and therefore help with whole-word reading (Pontart et al., 2013). Word-processed print does not provide these overt connections which assist children in producing phonetically-plausible words.

The fine motor skills required to type are not as demanding as those required for handwriting. However, there is a need to be able to isolate fingers, apply appropriate pressure and be able to visually transition accurately between the keyboard and the monitor/screen. These are skills which those who have visual-motor and visual-spatial integration difficulties find particularly problematic.

Word processing involves the **bilateral** co-ordination of two hands. It requires considerably less in-hand manipulation than handwriting, reducing opportunities for developing skills that can enhance individuals' ability to perform other activities requiring enhanced dexterity (such as manipulating buttons when dressing and undressing). Interestingly, recent research has suggested that the speed gained from two-handed typing can negatively affect the quality of writing, with less sophisticated vocabulary being used (Medimorec & Risko, 2016). In addition, the need to cross the midline, which is essential when writing, is not required when word processing. This can have a bearing on other skills requiring the transition across the body, such as the passing of a ball in sport, and scanning from left to write when reading.

It could be argued that word processing is faster than writing, and this may be true for some individuals. However, studies have found a high association between handwriting speed and typing speed. Therefore, individuals who struggle with automatic letter transcription fluency will also struggle with keyboarding (Connelly et al., 2007). We may then conclude that we should not relegate handwriting to a historic art just because technology is available and advanced.

If we all had Segways®, would we simply stop walking?
Rae Pica, 2011

Handwriting and the curriculum

The requirement to achieve the complexities of handwriting in the UK is demanded at a very young age. The Early Years Foundation Stage (EYFS) Profile (2014) and National Curriculum (2014) articulate the expectations that children should aspire to with regard to handwriting.

The EYFS Profile stipulates the following target for children under the age of five years old:

Early Learning Goal 10 – Writing
Children use their phonic knowledge to write words in ways which match their spoken sounds. They also write some irregular common words. They write simple sentences which can be read by themselves and others. Some words are spelt correctly and others are phonetically plausible.

Typical behaviours that relate to this learning goal are that the child:

- uses some clearly identifiable letters to communicate meaning, representing some sounds correctly and in sequence
- writes their own name and other things such as labels and captions
- attempts to write short sentences in meaningful context
- uses a pencil and holds it effectively to form recognisable letters, most of which are formed correctly.

The National Curriculum for children in Year 1 (aged 5–6 years), extends these skills further:

Pupils' writing during Year 1 will generally develop at a slower pace than their reading. This is because they need to encode the sounds they hear in words (spelling skills), develop the physical skill needed for handwriting, and learn how to organise their ideas in writing.

Programme of study (statutory requirements)	Notes and guidance (non-statutory)
Pupils should be taught to: 1 sit correctly at a table, holding a pencil comfortably and correctly 2 begin to form lower-case letters in the correct direction, starting and finishing in the right place 3 form capital letters 4 form digits 0–9 5 understand which letters belong to which handwriting 'families' (i.e. letters that are formed in similar ways) and to practise these.	Handwriting requires frequent and discrete, direct teaching. Pupils should be able to form letters correctly and confidently. The size of the writing implement (pencil, pen) should not be too large for a young pupil's hand. Whatever is being used should allow the pupil to hold it easily and correctly so that bad habits are avoided. Left-handed pupils should receive specific teaching to meet their needs.

To acquire such a range of skills at an early age demands time dedicated to direct teaching, together with a learning environment that provides opportunities for experimentation and practice. Curriculum planning needs to include Readiness to Write activities before writing is formally introduced. These are preparatory skills such as the formation of shapes, tracking activities and pencil manipulation tasks. These should be highly motivating and fun so that writing is not seen as being arduous and boring. The reality is that minimal focus is given to introducing these skills despite the fact that if children are given the opportunity to practise the early skills of handwriting, there is a higher chance of it becoming an automatic process, which is essential for later composition (McCarney et al., 2013).

Handwriting difficulties

The information and evidence outlined in this chapter demonstrates that handwriting is a very complex skill. It is evident that the Curriculum is highly aspirational in anticipating that children will be successful in acquiring this ability at such an early stage in their lives. The reality is that between 10–34% of school-aged children and young people struggle to succeed in many facets involved in the writing process. Given that approximately 30–50% of time in school involves handwriting-related tasks, it is no surprise that difficulties in this area can have long-lasting negative outcomes on individuals' self-confidence and self-esteem, and this may account for some of the behavioural and emotional issues seen by teachers in the classroom (Feder & Majnemer, 2007; Rosenblum et al., 2010).

I don't have bad handwriting. I have my own font.

The difficulties individuals experience in producing fast, legible script arise from anomalies in biomechanical, sensorimotor, perceptual and linguistic processes. These need to be examined in detail to determine the underlying processes involved in producing legible script before suggesting how difficulties can be addressed. There are many aspects of handwriting that commonly prove challenging to children and young people, including:

- posture for writing (core stability)
- pelvic and shoulder girdle stability
- the ability to cross the midline (i.e. to effectively travel across the page from left to right)
- hand dominance or preference
- letter formation
- understanding of uppercase and lowercase letters
- the ability to write or draw in a line or within margins
- grip and control of the pen(cil)
- positioning of the paper
- the ability to insert the appropriate amount of space between words
- orientation of letters
- transitioning from print to cursive writing
- combining motor co-ordination with composition and spelling
- regulating pressure through the pen(cil)
- organising writing on the page
- producing writing that is both legible and fast.

By examining the potential cause of the difficulties an individual has, it is possible to recommend the best way to remediate the issue. For example, poor letter formation may reflect inadequate form constancy (a vital precursor to many aspects of learning, affecting the ability to determine size and shape); a lack of fluency may indicate struggles with motor co-ordination or difficulties knowing where to join letters; an increase in pressure through the writing instrument may indicate poor **proprioceptive feedback** (the awareness of muscle position and pressure) or highlight ergonomic factors, such as the table being at an inappropriate height.

We need to examine both the product and process of handwriting to address handwriting difficulties. Initially, we need to evaluate the ergonomic and biomechanical influences on the motor actions demanded of handwriting, considering posture, positioning, handedness, manipulation, classroom furniture and writing tools. We then need to examine the foundation perceptual skills that are required in preparation for writing, exploring what happens when these have not been established.

Three specific approaches to addressing handwriting needs will be examined in this book:

1. The bottom-up or **process-orientated approach** which targets the underlying components of the handwriting process in order to improve legibility, fluency and speed.
2. The top-down or **task-specific approach** which identifies and targets specific handwriting presentation difficulties.
3. The **compensatory approach**, which introduces technology.

Finally, this book will provide an overview of handwriting assessments and how the data obtained from these can be used to establish outcomes which will determine an intervention. A series of Case studies will demonstrate how to take a sample of an individual's handwriting and analyse its components in order to determine aspects which need to be changed. They will suggest resources, strategies and interventions which can be used to enhance an individual's written presentation and output.

Recommendations will not only focus on individuals who have **dysgraphia** (a deficiency in the ability to write, primarily in terms of handwriting, but also coherence), but also those who may have neurological or musculo-skeletal differences that affect their written work (such as those with cerebral palsy, muscular dystrophy, autism, juvenile rheumatoid arthritis or limb deficiency).

> *His most blatant failure was in writing. This motorically clumsy child had atrocious handwriting. The pen did not obey him, it stuck and sputtered; he corrected without concern for appearance and would simply write new letters on top of old ones.*
> Asperger, 1944

CHAPTER 2
Ergonomic and biomechanical aspects of handwriting

The ergonomic and biomechanical aspects of producing written communication can cause some of the formational errors which render handwriting illegible. If the mechanics involved in controlling the pen(cil) are impeded by incorrect furniture and inappropriate writing tools, then fluency and automaticity will never be achieved. The recommendation to sit correctly and develop the right pen(cil) grip is often not supported by enough explanation as to *why* these are important in the writing process. An understanding of both the ergonomic and biomechanical aspects of handwriting provides the rationale for environment and furniture adjustments.

Ergonomics

Ergonomics is a science concerned with the 'fit' between people and their work and aims to make sure that the task, equipment, information and environment are appropriate for the individual. When applied to children, their handwriting is their 'work'. We must therefore consider the fit between the furniture (chair and desk), the writing tools (pen(cil) and paper) and the biomechanical demands of the task with respect to dexterity and in-hand manipulation skills.

It is not uncommon for primary-aged children who attend schools in the UK to be taught in mixed-age classes and this can be an issue when considering the ergonomics of the environment. For example, Reception and Year 1 children often share the same space and furniture despite the (often significant) difference between the height and size of an August-born four-year-old, and a September-born almost-six-year-old.

To ensure that each child sits in a position that optimises their handwriting skills, furniture will need to vary in size according to the height and postural needs of the individuals. A truly inclusive classroom will look messy as furniture will differ in sizes to accommodate the unique needs of each pupil.

Biomechanics

Biomechanics is a science concerned with the internal and external forces acting on the human body. When applied to handwriting, we must consider the pencil grip, manipulation of the pencil, and the regulation of movement from left to right across the paper. Non-proficient handwriting is a work activity characterised by 'inferior biomechanical ergonomics, handwriting quality, efficiency, and significantly different handwriting processes' (Rosenblum et al., 2006).

There are three biomechanical phases operating in the writing process:

1 The position of the hand and arm, and the grip on the pencil.
2 Gross and fine motor control (arm and finger movement).
3 The fluctuating speed and movement of the pencil, and the pauses caused by pencil lifts or wrist alterations (units of movement). Good and poor writers differ in the manner in which they divide the whole movement into units.

It is important to consider the ergonomic and biomechanical factors together in order to determine which facets are impacting on the individual's ability to produce legible handwriting. To do this we need to examine:

- chair and table height
- posture and limb stability
- the influence of primitive reflexes
- movement translation from left to right (involving midline crossing)
- the position of the arm and paper
- pressure through the writing instrument.

Chair and table height

To provide a secure base to effectively control the upper limbs, stability is required in the trunk and pelvis. Initially it is important to ensure that an individual's feet are placed firmly on the floor. The height of some classroom seats may leave younger or smaller children struggling to secure this position, resulting in them wrapping their feet around the chair legs, or virtually standing in order to write.

Ideally, the hips and knees should be at a 90º angle (Figure 1), with the height of the table reaching the base of the elbow when flexed (bent) to 90º. If the table height is too high, the shoulders will be hunched and the visual field will be too close to the wording and paper, causing perceptual disturbances. If the table is too low, the child will lean too far forward, increasing the pressure through the pen(cil) (Parush et al., 1998). A cut-out table (which has a semi-circular indent) can be used to provide more upper limb support in handwriting activities for those with cerebral palsy. This will allow the writer to rest their elbows on the table whilst maintaining an upright posture (Kavak & Bumin, 2009).

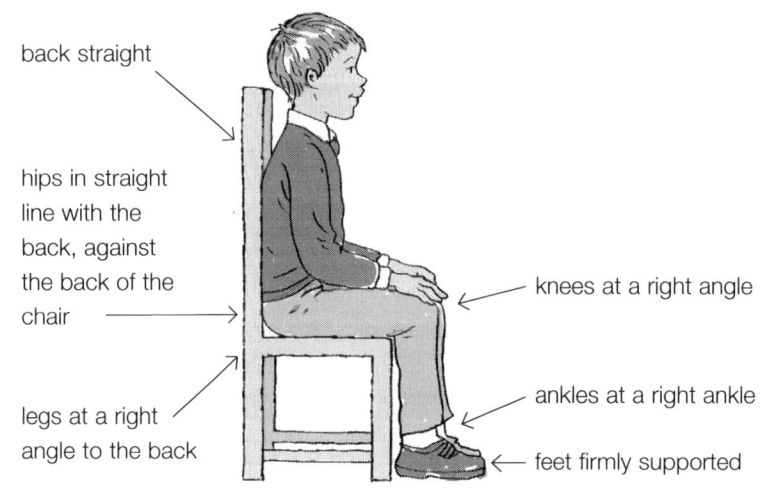

- back straight
- hips in straight line with the back, against the back of the chair
- legs at a right angle to the back
- knees at a right angle
- ankles at a right ankle
- feet firmly supported

Figure 1: Optimal position for writing

Some children and young people, especially those with cerebral palsy, may struggle to keep their feet on the floor. They may have a strong **extensor thrust** where their hips extend or stretch outward, causing the feet to slip forwards. This reduces stability and will affect upper limb control. To help with this, a TheraBand™ strap can be placed around the front two chair legs. Individuals' feet can be tucked behind the elasticated strap to prevent the extension of the legs (Figure 2).

Figure 2: Feet tucked behind TheraBand strap

There are certain occasions when the height of the table should be lowered if an individual is struggling to produce enough force through the pen(cil), resulting in lighter pressure and poor control and writing beginning to look 'spidery'. Again, this can be a particular issue with individuals who have cerebral palsy and struggle with increased extensor hip tone, causing them to extend back against their chair (Figure 3). In these situations, the table should be lowered by 4–6cm in order to tilt the trunk forward, so that the individual's body weight can increase the forward force and in doing so improve pressure and writing control.

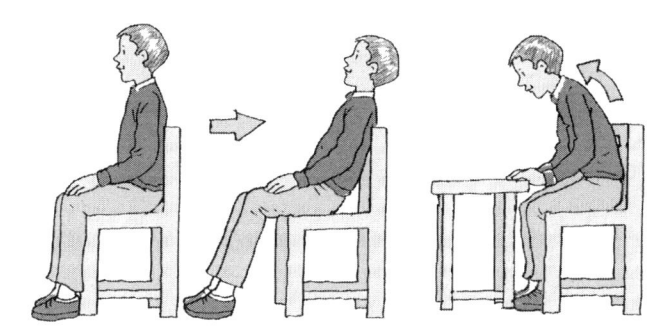

Figure 3: An extensor thrust can be rectified by slightly lowering the height of the table

If a chair or table is too high for an individual, foot blocks can be used to raise their feet position. In an ideal situation, adjustable furniture should be purchased so that its height can be modified according to individual need.

Posture and limb stability

Handwriting requires considerable stability in the upper body and shoulder girdle in order to control the movements of the upper limbs. This is not possible if the pelvic girdle, which is essential for maintaining a secure sitting position, is unstable. If this is the case, twisting and slouching positions are observed. Likewise, legibility can be affected by poor shoulder girdle stability. Some children have low muscle tone or lack steadiness in this area which negatively impacts on their handwriting and success in other fine motor tasks. There is also some evidence that the retention of early reflexes can have a bearing on positioning and posture when writing. It is therefore important that pelvic and shoulder stability and the influence of retained primitive reflexes on posture and tone are examined closely in individuals who struggle with handwriting.

Poor pelvic stability

The dexterity required to write demands that the lower trunk is well controlled and secure in order to maintain the position of the upper torso against gravity. Poor pelvic stability can result in slouching, twisting or too much forward lean, resulting in inconsistent pressure through the pen(cil) and affecting speed, output and legibility.

Placing the feet firmly on the floor is one way to improve this, but some children need a more dynamic longer-term solution which increases postural strength and requires their muscles to be active or work to maintain the stability around the pelvis. This can be achieved by replacing a conventional classroom chair with a stool or therapy ball, or by placing a core disc cushion on the chair's seat (Haan, 2015). The effort needed to maintain this position requires the muscles around the pelvic girdle to constantly adjust and adapt in order to maintain an effective sitting position (Figure 4).

Figure 4: Sitting on a therapy ball works the muscles around the pelvis

Another way to improve pelvic stability (as well as core stability) is to incorporate activities that develop the muscles around the lower back and hips into classroom and PE lessons and break time games. Activities such as crab football, floor football and seated volleyball strengthen the pelvis muscles to help the individual's sitting position become more stable. See Appendix A for further suggestions. This reiterates the fact that improving handwriting involves improving whole-body control, rather than simply practising tabletop pen(cil) and paper activities.

Poor shoulder stability

The ability to steady the shoulder girdle is also vital for effective pencil control. The initiation of dexterity required to manipulate a pencil demands the inhibition (or prevention) of joint movements at the wrist, elbow and shoulder. Shoulder girdle instability results in inappropriate pressure being placed through the pen(cil) and inaccurate dexterity.

Children occasionally have difficulties in this area. Sometimes this is because they have missed out on the developmental milestone of crawling, which typically occurs between 7–9 months of age. There is some evidence that the omission of crawling can affect pencil grip in five- and six-year old children (Rosenblum & Josman, 2003; Clearfield, 2004; Visser & Franzsen, 2010). Children will usually crawl for approximately 4–6 months before walking, and this provides important strength and muscle feedback through the shoulders. It also enhances the development of a body schema, and supports motor planning, visual perception, midline crossing and hand–eye co-ordination.

Research does not suggest that all is lost for those who did or do not crawl; rather, it highlights the importance of increasing their strength around the shoulder girdle in order to write effectively, by means of incorporating specific activities into PE and other lessons. For example, introduce wheelbarrow races, scooter board activities (Figure 5) and other crawling tasks to increase the strength in the upper limbs, as well as static resistance activities such as cave writing in art or history classes (Figure 6). This is a fun activity whereby paper is fixed to the underside of a table, and the child writes from a supine position. See Appendix B for more activity ideas for improving shoulder stability.

Figure 5: Scooter board activities increase shoulder girdle stability

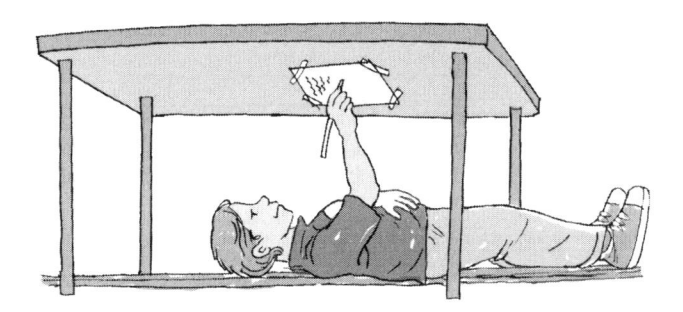

Figure 6: Cave writing

Influence of primitive reflexes

There is some evidence that poor posture can be also be caused by the poor inhibition and continued presence of primitive reflexes (Goddard-Blythe, 2005; Jordan-Black, 2005; Tarnai, 2012; Desorbay, 2013). Motor development commences in the mother's womb where early movements, often described by mothers as 'kicks', signal the start of a baby's movement. In fact, these are a series of basic (primitive) reflexes which are inhibited or suppressed just before or shortly after birth, making way for more advanced motor reactions such as protective or saving reactions (these are spontaneous responses to a situation; for example, if a child rocks or topples to the side or front, they will automatically reach out their arms to save or protect themselves from harm) before the child begins to develop more organised and deliberate motor control.

Occasionally these early reflexes remain, causing anomalies in posture, positioning and sitting control. Three of these primitive reflexes *may* have a particular bearing on handwriting:

1 Asymmetrical tonic neck reflex (ATNR)
2 Symmetrical tonic neck reflex (STNR) in prone
3 Spinal galant reflex

Asymmetrical tonic neck reflex (ATNR)

The ATNR is also called the 'fencer' reflex, due to the fact that when lying on their back, a very young baby (between 0–5 months old) adopts a fencing position. This reflex can be seen when a baby turns their head to one side, simultaneously extending or straightening the arm and the leg on the same side whilst bending or flexing the arm and hip on the opposite side. If their head turns to the right, the right arm will automatically extend; if the head turns to the left, the left arm will extend (Figure 7).

The ATNR should be inhibited or suppressed by the time the baby reaches 6–11 months of age.

Figure 7: ATNR, or 'fencer' reflex

Children who maintain this reflex will struggle to crawl as it will be difficult for them to straighten both arms in a forward direction at the same time, making it very difficult to control the reciprocal movement of outstretched arms. These children may spend time bottom-shuffling or commando crawling before learning to walk, gaining support through one supportive arm or none at all.

If the ATNR reflex is maintained, children will struggle to develop central symmetry and maintain a midline position. When working on a centrally-placed task, you will see them holding their head at an angle to see their work when writing. Tracking from left to right may also be problematic, and the child may appear to sit in a twisted position (Figure 8).

Figure 8: Continued presence of the ATNR affecting writing posture

Symmetrical tonic neck reflex (STNR) in prone

The STNR also has a bearing on posture and handwriting. It is a reflex which also occurs before a child starts to crawl.

If a baby is held in a prone position (i.e. looking downwards) carefully supported under their tummy, when the head extends back, the hips will flex or bend and the arms will stretch out (Figure 9). When the head bends forward, the arms will flex (Figure 10). This should be inhibited by the time the child is approximately 9–11 months old, so that they are able to crawl.

Figure 9: STNR extension 　　　　　　　　**Figure 10: STNR flexion**

The persistence of this reflex causes a child to slump forward onto their desk (Figure 11) because when they lower their head to look at their writing, this will automatically trigger their arms to bend and hips to slump forward.

Figure 11: Continued presence of the STNR affecting writing posture

To reduce the effects of both the ATNR and the STNR, it is vital that the height of the table and chair are correct. The height of the table should be increased slightly if the child is constantly slumping forward. The addition of a writing board will ensure that an upright posture is maintained and improve visual acuity (Figure 12).

Figure 12: An angled desk or angled writing board can improve posture and visual acuity

Spinal galant reflex

The spinal galant reflex can be seen in newborn babies up until 9–12 months of age. If the baby is gently stroked on their lower back to one side of the spine, the arm and hip on the same side will flex. The same will be true if the opposite side is stroked (Figure 13). The child appears to squirm towards the side that has been touched.

Figure 13: Spinal galant reflex

The continued presence of this reflex will cause a child to wriggle and writhe when anything touches their spine. The child may seem to be constantly on the move when they are expected to sit still, and may only settle when sitting in an unconventional position as the back of the chair stimulates the movement (Figure 14). The solution is to reduce contact with the spine by allowing the child to sit on a stool or therapy ball, which removes the trigger to the response.

Figure 14: Continued presence of the spinal galant reflex affecting writing posture

There are longer-term intervention programmes which aim to inhibit the imposing reflexes in order to improve motor control. *Primary Movement, The Institute of Neuro-Physiological Psychology (INPP) Developmental Exercise programme,* and *HANDLE* are three of these which have demonstrated some evidence of success in the early years (Jordan-Black, 2005; Goddard Blythe, 2009; Brown, 2010; Calcott, 2012).

Movement translation from left to right

An essential biomechanical element of writing in English is the ability to move the arm across the body from left to right. This requires the ability to cross the midline of the body, a skill that emerges when a baby is between 18–20 weeks old (Scharoun, 2014). The midline is the invisible line that divides the body into a left and right side. Effective crossing of the midline (or **contralateral reaching**) allows the child to sit still when seated at a desk and reach from one side of the paper to another to write from left to right without turning their bodies or paper. This is an important skill for the development of reading and writing (Smith, 2013). When crossing the midline, new neural pathways develop between the hemispheres of the brain, thus increasing an individual's overall functioning and learning experience (De Beer, 2015).

Some children and young people struggle to cross this midline position and it has been suggested that this not only affects writing posture, but may also result in problems with perceptual-motor development (Michell & Wood, 1999).

When a child is unable to cross the midline you will observe them:

- swapping their pen(cil) from one hand to another across the page
- moving their whole body with their hand across the page in a twisting motion (Figure 15)
- constantly trying to re-position their paper effectively (Figure 16)
- having difficulties scanning from left to right across the page when reading, frequently losing their place
- struggling to organise their writing on the page.

Figure 15: This child has shifted his body over to the left so his right hand does not have to reach over to work on his left side

Figure 16: This child has turned the paper sideways so she can write from bottom to top instead of reaching over to her left side with her right hand

To help achieve this skill, activities that involve midline crossing tasks should be included in the school day. These may include passing a ball in PE (Figure 17), catching a ball from a sideways position, country dancing, circle time activities, practising large lazy eights and other large movements (Figure 18), or blackboard activities.

Figure 17: Passing relay

Figure 18: Lazy eights

Bilateral activities involving the integrated use of both hands will also help. These can include using scissors, sewing, woodwork and cookery tasks.

Position of the arm and paper

A further ergonomic and biomechanical factor which affects the quality of handwriting is the position of the paper in relation to the arm. Some children place their paper square onto the table, aligned to the table edge. This causes an individual to write with their elbow pressed firmly against the side of their body, restricting the movement of the arm and subsequent writing fluency. It also causes the alignment of writing to change to a more upright position and reduces flow and speed. There are three particular reasons why children may do this:

1. They have been told to place their paper or book in this position.
2. They are 'fixing' their arm to the side of their body to obtain a secure position from which to control the paper.
3. They are tactile defensive (i.e. they have a sensory processing issue which affects their posture and positioning).

Teacher direction

Often, teachers believe that the writing paper or workbook is best aligned according to the position of the desk or table. This is often to counteract children who turn their page to a virtually horizontal position and write in an upwards direction if right-handed, or a towards-body direction if left-handed. These children will look as though their body is uncomfortably twisted and therefore guidance has good intentions.

The anatomical position of our arms is interesting in that when we bend our arms, they do not point forward as is assumed; rather, they create an angle to an invisible point located approximately 15cm ahead of our fingertips. It is therefore advisable to recommend that the paper or workbook is aligned to this angle to optimise the writer's working position. This can be encouraged by the use of a piece of thin Dycem® matting which has been marked with the ideal paper angle. This can be supplemented by identifying where the child should place their non-preferred hand to support the paper when writing.

Fixing the arm to the side of the body

Many children and young people will position their paper centrally so that they can 'fix' or secure their elbow against the side of their body. This produces the stability and security needed to write when the shoulder girdle is weak or muscle tone is low. This is particularly common in children with Down syndrome, ataxia, or those with a tremor, and is often apparent in children with developmental co-ordination disorder (DCD). These individuals' lack of stability around the shoulders means that writing can only be produced in a controlled manner if another part of the arm is stabilised; in this case, the elbow.

A solution to this is to increase the stability of the shoulder girdle through activities like those referred to in Appendix B, or to provide additional proprioceptive feedback (and subsequent stability) by providing additional weight to the forearm and wrist (Vishnu & Rekha, 2015). This can be achieved by purchasing a weighted wristband or forearm weights which provide the deep pressure missing for those with tremor or low muscle tone (Figure 19). The added weight reduces the need to fixate against the body, freeing the arm to develop more fluent script. This does not completely solve the underlying problem; however, it does enable the child to gain the necessary proprioceptive and motor feedback required to develop the foundational writing skills.

Figure 19: Use of forearm weights

Tactile defensiveness

Some children secure their arms against the sides of their bodies as tightly as possible because they have a sensory anomaly known as tactile defensiveness. These children cannot tolerate the possibility of light touch and, as a consequence, make their base of support and body position as narrow and tight as possible. For these children, light touch can be painful, feeling like a scratch on sunburnt skin. If they are tactile defensive, reactions will also be seen during other activities. For example, the child may be reluctant to stand in line for lunch, being concerned that they may be touched unexpectedly; they may lash out at a child who unexpectedly brushes past them; or they may be a fussy eater, being particularly intolerant of foods with certain textures (e.g. minced meat). Consideration will need to be given to whether there is a pattern of behaviours before an appropriate solution is found.

One quick and easy response to this problem is to allow the child to sit on a double desk alone, in a position where other children do not regularly need to pass. Gradually, the child will become less anxious and will develop a more appropriate, functional writing position. Longer-term solutions can be found in stimulating the deeper touch receptors through massage and activities requiring an increase in pressure through the limbs (e.g. rolling pastry or claywork). This will reduce the individual's sensitivity to light touch to a certain extent, allowing them to adopt a more relaxed writing position (Bhopti & Brown, 2013).

Pressure through the writing instrument

The quality of handwriting can be affected by the pressure or force placed through the pen(cil). This can also influence speed and fluency. Some children apply very little pressure and their writing appears light, poorly-formed and spidery; others will press so heavily that the paper tears or punctures.

The key determinants of force variability are pen(cil) grip and the regulation of proprioception. The next chapter will explore pen(cil) grip in more detail, but first it is necessary to consider how the positioning and alteration of furniture can alter anomalies in downward force through the pen(cil).

Proprioception provides our position sense and regulates pressure. There are a wide number of **mecanoreceptors** located in our joints, tendons and muscles (such as Pacinian corpuscles, Golgi tendon organs and muscle spindles) which provide us with information about our joints' angle, muscle stretch and tension, and the position of the limb in relation to the body. These receptors also help to determine pressure placed through our limbs.

When writing, proprioceptors allow us to accurately adjust the pressure through the writing tool, be this pen or pencil, enabling us to write in a fluent manner. The refinement of this adjustment can be appreciated more when using a ballpoint pen. When the ink does not appear to be as free-flowing as usual, extra force stimulates a smoother flow of ink or indicates the need for a change of pen.

Some of the difficulties seen when children and young people press too hard or too little through the pen(cil) can be attributed to poor regulation of the proprioceptive system. Children with DCD, Down syndrome, cerebral palsy, attention deficit hyperactivity disorder (ADHD), autism spectrum condition (ASC) or low muscle tone may experience this lack of proprioceptive sensitivity. This will often cause them to apply more pressure in order to experience the correct feedback through the muscles. This can result in broken pencil nibs and a subsequent reduction in written output.

Some children produce too little force through the pen(cil), making their writing appear light and difficult to read. This is often caused by poor positioning of the wrist when writing, with the wrist being lifted off the page, resulting in poorer pencil control. It can also be caused by poor writing posture which causes the child to extend backwards, controlling the pencil with a whole-arm movement rather than the fingers and wrist, with stability provided by the forearm.

Both heavy pressure with excessive force and light pressure with poor arm positioning affect the quality and quantity of handwriting and therefore need to be addressed. Many children and young people need assistance to receive the correct feedback through the muscles, and then to learn how to self-regulate pressure to write more effectively. The use of pelvic and shoulder girdle stability activities (see Appendices A and B) has been found to improve proprioceptive sensitivity, although this may be for a limited period of time (Kane & Bell, 2009; Menz et al., 2013). In addition, dynamic activities (including resistance games incorporated into PE lessons) can also enhance proprioception. These include games such as tug of war and wheelbarrow races.

The use of Catchabubbles (a bubble solution which makes bubbles that turn into a fine plastic when airbound) can help young children regulate the pressure placed through their fingertips (Figure 20). The bubbles can be caught or stomped on depending on the skill needing to be taught. It is advisable to play with these outside, where games can be introduced to either increase or reduce pressure through the hand and fingertips.

Figure 20: Catchabubbles

The activities below use Catchabubbles to regulate pressure through the limbs and can actively promote hand–eye co-ordination.

Sensory bubbles activities

Aim: Improve hand–eye co-ordination

Blow bubbles and ask children to try to catch them on the end of each of their fingers.

Aim: To improve proprioceptive feedback (to reduce pressure)

Blow bubbles and ask children to collect as many as possible on their hands. The winner is the child with the most bubbles.

Aim: To improve proprioceptive feedback (to increase pressure)

Blow bubbles and see how many children can catch them, swipe them and squash them with a clap.

Aim: Precision

Blow bubbles and ask children to try to make a tower of bubbles on the end of one finger.

Aim: Body awareness

Blow bubbles, then call out a part of the body (e.g. nose, little finger, elbow) and ask children to try to catch a bubble on that body part.

Aim: Pinch

Blow bubbles and ask children to catch and squash them using a pinching motion.

Teaching the self-regulation of pressure using feedback through the use of a light-up pen can also improve fluency. These are pens with an LED at the end which is illuminated if the right pressure is applied. Children and young people can be challenged to reduce the force through the pen so that the light does not come on, or be encouraged to keep the light on whilst writing, depending on the desired objective.

Another way to develop pressure regulation is through the use of a carbonated paper pad in which layers of carbonated paper are interspersed with ordinary paper. Individuals are then challenged to send a message to another person. If they tend to press on the pen(cil) too hard, they should be challenged to reduce the pressure so that their text is translated onto only two sheets of paper. If they need to press on harder, they should be challenged to send a message to three people at one time, increasing the pressure so that their writing is translated onto three sheets of paper.

There is now software (such as the Wacom Cintiq 12WX) which can provide feedback on how much pressure is placed through a stylus pen when using a tablet. Although this is good for self-regulation, there is a difference in the friction of writing on a tablet with a plastic stylus to writing on paper with a pen(cil). However, it can give a reasonable indication of how much force an individual places through a pen(cil).

The use of weighted forearm and wrist cuffs can also regulate the force an individual exerts through a pen(cil) by enhancing proprioceptive feedback (Priya & Rekha, 2015). The addition of an angled writing board will also ensure that the wrist keeps in contact with the working surface, providing a stable base from which to write.

An alternative to the use of a weighted forearm cuff is to weight the writing tool itself. It is possible to purchase weighted pens or to add weights to pencils (Figure 21). These fit onto most standard pens and pencils, and are kept in place by simple O-rings. The weight increases feedback and proprioception so individuals have more awareness of their hand and fingers, resulting in greater control. Weighted pencils are also particularly beneficial for children who have poor sensory processing, including children with DCD.

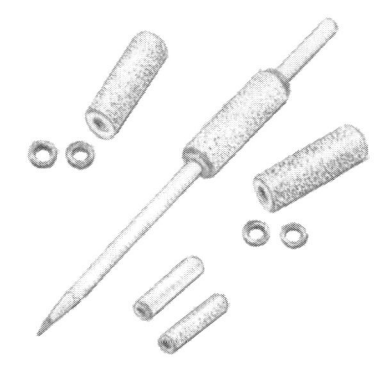

Figure 21: Weighted pen and weights to attach to pen(cil)s

These recommendations will help the writer to apply the correct amount of pressure through the writing instrument, particularly children who have cerebral palsy who may struggle to accommodate fluctuating postural tone.

Summary

This chapter has explained the importance of the biomechanical and ergonomic factors involved in the process of writing and has demonstrated how the classroom environment and its furniture play a part in the effective production of legible script. This is supported by evidence that pupils who are accommodated with dimensionally-suitable furniture have better body posture and can produce more readable text at an improved speed than those who are struggling with the height of their desk and/or chair. The height, shape and position of an individual's desk and chair therefore have implications for good posture and biomechanical and functional success (Gonçalves & Arezes, 2012).

Further evidence demonstrates that pupils who struggle with handwriting show significant differences with respect to all the ergonomic and biomechanical factors, including body positioning, pressure adjustment, crossing the midline and the adjustment of force through the writing instrument, compared to those who don't struggle with the skill (Smith-Zuzovsky & Exner, 2004; Rosenblum et al., 2006). An important biomechanical and ergonomic issue not addressed in this chapter is that of hand dominance and the development of an appropriate pen(cil) grip. The following chapter is dedicated to this topic.

CHAPTER 3
Handedness and pen(cil) grip

Writing is a unilateral fine motor skill which requires fine-tuning of finger position to manipulate a pen(cil). However, many of the difficulties experienced in accomplishing this skill are attributed to hand preference and anomalies in how the child or young person holds the pen(cil), and its subsequent impact on manipulation. This chapter will examine handedness and pen(cil) grip in more detail to determine whether these designations are real or perceived.

Handedness

We will start by considering the issue of hand preference (known as handedness or hand dominance), identifying questions which are often asked by teachers and parents alike:

- How do you determine which hand an individual should write with?
- Does it matter if a child swaps hands when they write?
- Do left-handers have more handwriting difficulties than right-handers?
- Why do some individuals write with one hand but perform other activities with the other?
- Do left-handers need different teaching techniques to those used for right-handers?
- Are left-handers more prone to mirror writing and producing letter inversions and reversals than right-handers?

Hand preference can usually be identified at a very early age, with a clear inclination seen by the time a child reaches 18 months old. However, many children swap from hand to hand for many years and do not demonstrate a preference until they are aged between 4–6 years. Indeed, Evans (2014) found that 100% of the total sample of 50 children in his research were found to display at least some elements of cross-lateral preference at the age of 4–5 years old (e.g. they preferred to use their left hand for pre-writing tasks, and right foot for playing football). These figures support the notion that a true sidedness may take considerably longer to develop than originally thought.

The majority of the population are right-handed and approximately 10% prefer to use their left hand. This is primarily determined by genetics. In addition, some individuals are cross-lateral, meaning that they may prefer to lead with their right foot and write with their left hand, or vice versa. Approximately 1% are ambidextrous, able to use both hands with equal proficiency. Others have mixed dominance, continuing to swap hand, eye, foot and ear preference throughout their lives. These individuals can prove more challenging when teaching handwriting.

There are two ways that handedness can be determined. The dominant hand is that which either:

- performs faster or more precisely on manual tests, or
- an individual prefers to use, regardless of performance.

It is possible to determine an individual's preference using the following laterality table.

		Activity	Left	Right
Hand	1	Ask the individual to pick up a pencil placed in a central position on a table. Which hand do they use?		
	2	Ask the individual to unscrew a bottle top. The more dominant hand will undertake the twisting action.		
	3	Ask the individual to clap out a tune. The dominant hand will tend to be on top and be the most active.		
Ear	4	Tell the individual you are going to whisper something secret in their ear. Which ear do they turn towards you?		
	5	Provide a ticking watch or conch shell and ask the individual to listen to the sound. Which ear do they use to listen to the sound?		
Foot	6	Ask the individual to climb a small flight of stairs. Which foot do they lead from?		
	7	Ask the individual to kick a football into a goal. Which foot do they use to achieve this?		
	8	Ask the individual to march like a soldier. Which foot do they lead from?		
Eye	9	Ask the individual to look through a kaleidoscope or a rolled-up piece of paper. Which eye do they use?		
	10	Cut out a peephole in a piece of card. Ask the individual to look through the hole. Which eye do they use?		

Right-sided preference: agreement mostly on the right column (6 or more)

Left-sided preference: agreement mostly on the left column (6 or more)

Ambidextrous: equal use of either hand, foot, ear or eye

Cross-lateral: use of right eye/left foot or left foot/right eye

Mixed dominance: inconsistency in hand use and swapping is apparent continuously, even when performing the same task

See the accompanying CD-ROM for a printable copy of this table.

Left-hand dominance

There used to be considerable stigma attached to being left-handed, to the extent that children were forced into using their right hand for unilateral activities such as handwriting. Some of these negative connotations are unknowingly referred to today, with less attachment to the use of the left hand. For example, the French word *gauche* means *left*, but is also used to represent clumsiness, as is the expression *'he has two left feet'* when referring to someone who cannot dance very well.

Interestingly, many left-handed children write using this hand, but attempt other fine motor tasks with their right. This is often due to the fact that as the majority of the population are right-handed, the preponderance of tools such as scissors, tin openers, pens and peelers are designed to reflect the strength in the right hand, therefore providing those who are left-handed with little choice other than to practise skills using their right hand.

When writing in English, there are unique difficulties faced by those who are left-handed. Right-handers are able to 'pull' the pencil across the page from left to right, whereas a left-hander must write towards their body, 'pushing' the pencil in the process. The writing is occluded by the writing hand affecting the overall view of written presentation, and the writing hand smudges work produced in ink and soft lead.

To accommodate this, some left-handers adopt a hooked grip (Figure 22), limiting the amount of pressure that can be applied through the pencil and causing wrist cramps and fatigue. They may also rotate their paper to improve the visual field, making their posture appear twisted and uncomfortable.

Figure 22: Hooked grip

To help with this, their paper should be placed at an angle with the top left corner angled upwards (rotated 45º clockwise) so that the paper is in alignment with the angle of the arm. The introduction of an angled writing board can be effective in improving visual acuity, preventing the twisting posture (Figure 12). A thin layer of Dycem® non-stick matting will help to maintain the paper's position.

An often overlooked but simple resolution to the issue of awkward positioning often adopted by those who are left-handed is to ensure that they are always positioned on the left side of a desk when sharing with a right-hander to prevent bumping, or to provide them with a double desk of their own to provide them with more space in which to develop a functional writing posture.

Left-handed children and young people should be encouraged to hold their pen(cil) a little higher up the shaft than right-handers (at approximately 3–4cm above the nib) so that they can see the nib more clearly. If they forget, loops of elastic or Loom Bands can be added to the pen(cil) to remind them of the appropriate positioning. The right hand should serve to anchor the page. If using a pencil, a harder lead (e.g. HB) is less likely to smudge.

Initially, it can be helpful for left-handed individuals to practise letter shapes using chalk on a blackboard so that errors can be rubbed out easily. The friction of the chalk on a blackboard also produces tiny vibrations which stimulate the muscles of the hand and upper arm. This helps the kinaesthetic memory recall the movements needed to produce letter shapes. The blackboard can also be wall-mounted to improve individuals' shoulder stability.

Letter formation is the same for both left- and right-handers, but care must be taken to observe the writer orientating the letters correctly. There may be a tendency for left-handers to reverse the orientation of the letter *o*, leading to difficulties when joining letters. As left-handers will 'pull' their writing across the page, it can sometimes be more effective to allow them to cross their *t*s and *f*s from right to left rather than vice versa. This will reduce the likelihood of tearing the paper when pushing from left to right. However, the ideal is for the individual to create shapes and lines in the direction of flow, which is left to right, and this should be encouraged whenever possible.

It is possible to purchase a *Letter formation guide for left-handed children* from www.lefthandedchildren.org to help those who are left-handed form their letters appropriately. Left-handed pens and pencils can also be purchased to make the writing process more comfortable and free-flowing, and left-handed writing programmes can be useful in establishing early skills. These programmes include:

- *Writing left-handed... write in, not left out* by Mark Stewart (National Handwriting Association)
- *Left hand writing skills* by Mark & Heather Stewart (Robinswood Press)
- *Your left-handed child: making things easy for left-handers in a right-handed world* by Lauren Milsom (Hamlyn Publishers)

Famous left-handers	
Barack Obama	Aristotle
Leonardo Da Vinci	Bill Gates
David Bowie	Lady Gaga
Prince William	Winston Churchill
Paul McCartney	Natalie Cole
Steve Jobs	Helen Keller
Tom Cruise	Marie Curie

A further assumption made about those who are left-handed is that they are more likely to mirror-write or produce inverted and reversed letter shapes than their right-handed peers, owing to their supposed differences in perception. This is in fact a myth, and both right- and left-handed children may struggle to accurately orientate letters (Fischer & Koch, 2016).

Ambidexterity

Being ambidextrous can be a great asset, and many professionals who require considerable dexterity in both hands for their work (e.g. surgeons) may overtly train their non-dominant hand to become more proficient. When children are ambidextrous, it is often the case that they choose to write using their right hand, probably due to easier access to right-handed equipment (Vuoksima et al., 2009).

Although being ambidextrous is a unique skill which will be beneficial for word processing (which involves bilateral skills), writing remains a unilateral activity. Therefore, it is important to encourage the use of the same hand during a child's early years when this new motor skill is being learned. Initially, control of a pen(cil) may be less polished and the execution of the action may be slower in an ambidextrous child because the muscle groups involved are poorly co-ordinated due to the sharing of motor co-ordination between limbs for pre-writing play. However, with practice, proficiency in using both hands will gradually improve.

The advantages of encouraging unilaterality are:

- Children can learn to manipulate objects in a predominantly consistent way, resulting in greater skill and efficiency.
- Children can develop refined dexterity and precision in a specific hand, resulting in a more efficient manipulation of tools and objects.
- Children can develop more accurate aim-directed movements.

Controversially, some theorists believe that there is no such thing as having two dominant hands. Others believe that it can have a negative effect on the individual. For example, one study of ambidextrous school-aged children suggested that they may be more likely to have mental health, language and academic problems than their peers because their dominant hand has not been established, causing confusion in the brain (Bryner, 2010).

Many texts confuse cross-laterality and mixed dominance. A distinction must be made between these preferences. **Cross-laterality** describes a child who may consistently use their right hand but prefer to kick a football using their left leg, or they may have a preference for using their right eye but prefer to use their left ear for more careful listening tasks. **Mixed dominance** describes a child who regularly alternates between using their right and left hand, or right and left foot, ear and eye; presenting with less refined control and efficiency.

Cross-laterality

Many children are cross-lateral in their early years before establishing a definite preference from the age of six years onwards; others continue to have cross-lateral preferences into adulthood, developing extremely proficient motor control. It has been suggested that cross-laterality can be a positive development. For example, a study of children's literacy and dominant side (Marmoth, 2013) demonstrated that:

- right-eye dominance appears to be associated with literacy skill advantage
- left-ear dominance also appears to be associated with literacy skill advantage
- collectively, children with the profile of left-brain, right-eye and left-ear dominance scored the highest (on average) in phonological awareness, spelling, reading and literacy.

Initially, cross-lateral children may have difficulties deciding which their preferred hand for writing is, but when it is established they are consistent in their use throughout their lives.

One question teachers and parents often ask is how to determine which hand they should encourage a child to use. There are two strategies which can help practitioners to decide which hand to encourage the child to use when learning the initial movements of writing. The first is to complete the laterality table provided in this chapter (page 24).

The second requires more discernment. Provide the child with a double-sided blackboard of approximately 1m², depending on the age of the child (children younger than six years old may need a smaller board of 75cm²). Position it so that the board edge is facing the child (Figure 23). Give them two pieces of chalk, one in either hand, and encourage the child to practise a series of patterns using both hands together, starting closely to the body and moving away towards the opposite edge of the board.

Figure 23: The use of a double-sided blackboard to determine handedness

The following patterns can be used:

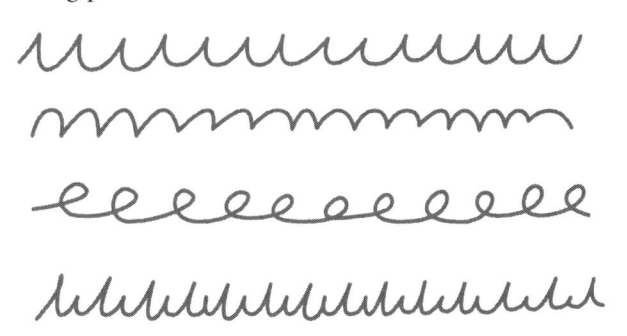

Practise these repetitions for five minutes three times per day for approximately a week. The child or young person will not be able to see their patterns. At the end of the week, review the patterns produced and identify those which appear more fluent and consistently sized. This should indicate the hand that the child should be encouraged to write with. This is usually clear for a cross-lateral individual. If there is very little difference in presentation, consider whether the child is ambidextrous or has mixed dominance.

Other recommendations for identifying which hand a child should use for writing include the use of **hand dynamometer tests** which analyse the strength and power in each hand, or tests which involve performing a series of tasks such as using scissors, opening jars and unscrewing nuts and bolts. Alternatively, evidence-based assessments such as the WatHand Box Test (Bryden et al., 2000) can be used. This asks participants to perform a series of tasks (such as tossing a ball) and records which hand is used for each task. It then produces a laterality quotient by subtracting the number of times the left hand is used from the number of times the right hand is used and dividing that by the number of tasks performed (Gruber et al., 2012).

Mixed dominance

This refers to those children and young people whose preference for using one side or the other swaps continually, in every activity, on a daily basis. Some psychologists believe that this is an indicator of neurological problems, minimal brain damage or developmental delay (Orton, 1937; Erdhardt, 2012). Mixed dominance indicates a poorly-established hemispherical dominance, with these children having particular difficulties with letter orientation, reading and organising the sequence of letters to produce words. It is also suggested that these children have greater difficulty than others in crossing the body midline, so the child may be observed swapping hands to complete a task that requires this skill (Evans, 2014).

Mixed dominance can sometimes present in those with dyslexia, slow processing skills, poor attention or concentration, poor spatial planning or organisation, delayed language and/or learning difficulties (Hauck & Dewey, 2001; Markoulakis et al., 2012). It can also affect motor co-ordination. Tan (1985) found that children who lacked a definite hand preference obtained significantly lower scores on motor abilities tests than others and concluded that children who establish hand preference early are better co-ordinated than those who establish hand preference late or not at all. This affects the motor co-ordination involved in producing legible script.

Interestingly, it has been found that many children and young people with autism are more prone to mixed dominance during their early years, and later adopt a left-handed preference. This is significant in that language is a highly lateralised function. This means that the majority of people use the left hemisphere of their brain to process language, and are usually right-handed. If language delays and impairments are linked to inconsistent or mixed dominance, then there is a possibility that delays in acquiring a specific dominance could be used to indicate a possible language delay or difference, giving the potential for earlier diagnosis and intervention implementation (Lindell & Hudry, 2013; Rysstad & Pedersen, 2015).

For those who appear to have mixed dominance, the aforementioned strategies should be used to determine a preferred sidedness. This will provide a basis from which a teacher can encourage the child or young person to write.

Writing using the non-dominant hand

There are occasions when it is necessary to teach a child or young person to write using their non-dominant hand. Children may have a hemiplegia or hemiparesis (one-sided weakness) due to cerebral palsy, stroke or an acquired brain injury. Some may have complete functional loss of their dominant hand due to Erb's palsy, nerve paralysis or chronic juvenile arthritis. Others may have been born with a missing limb or digits or experienced an amputation. These individuals will need to learn how to write with their non-dominant hand, which poses a considerable challenge.

It may seem a more feasible option to teach these individuals how to use a keyboard rather than write; however, the positive effects of learning to write will not be realised if they are immediately introduced to a keyboard and taught to type in their early years. Although typing will produce legible text, the essential skills gained through learning to control a pen(cil) and create letter forms will be reduced. Encouraging a child to write using a non-dominant limb will not only help them with visual recognition of letter forms and the linguistic understanding of how these connect to produce words, but will also enhance dexterity to enable the individual to tackle other one-handed tasks such as unbuttoning shirts, making a sandwich, pouring a drink or manipulating materials.

Practice is key. Research has shown that children and young people who are strongly encouraged to use their non-dominant limb to write and who undertake extensive repetition and rehearsal can ultimately achieve nearly comparable levels of skill to that of their dominant hand (Philip & Frey, 2014).

There are some specific interventions which can help to develop dexterity and control in the non-dominant limb:

- *Write from the Start: perceptuo-motor writing programme* by Ion Teodorescu & Lois Addy (LDA). This has been used with adults who have experienced a stroke and needed to learn how to write again using their non-dominant limb. The initial results proved positive.
- *Handwriting for Heroes* (Yancosek et al., 2015). This is a writing programme developed by an American occupational therapist for war veterans who have lost a dominant upper limb due to armed conflict. It is a task-orientated workbook that teaches writing with the non-preferred hand through the repetition of increasingly complex writing tasks and patterns. This programme has been shown to be effective in teaching children how to use their non-dominant limb for writing, with results seen within six weeks (Yancosek et al., 2012).

Pen(cil) grip

Once handedness has been determined, we need to analyse how the hand works in order to identify a dynamic, effective writing grip to successfully produce legible script.

The hand contains an intricate network of 35 muscles which work together to provide the dexterity required to write at speed and the endurance required to write for prolonged periods of time. The incredible biomechanical intricacies of muscles, ligaments and joints work in combination with ergonomically-designed writing tools to allow the functional movements of handwriting to be realised.

The amazing human hand contains:
- 28 major and minor bones (including the sesamoid bone)
- 29 major joints
- 123 named ligaments
- 35 muscles which move the fingers and thumb (17 intrinsic muscles originate in the palm and 18 extrinsic muscles originate in the forearm)
- 48 named nerves
- 30 named arteries

In the UK, we initially begin to mark-make during early childhood using chalk, wax crayons and paint, progressing on to pencils when handwriting is formally introduced. When the use of pencils becomes automatic, we encourage the use of a biro, rollerball, fibretip or fountain pen. It is therefore important to ask why we use this approach. Why do we teach children to write using a pencil rather than a pen? Why don't we introduce them to a rollerball or biro in their early years? After all, isn't writing in pen less effortful than writing in pencil?

The answer to this lies in the question. Writing with a pencil is indeed more effortful and this serves an important purpose. The friction of pencil lead against paper provides tiny vibrations which stimulate proprioceptors located in the joints, muscles and tendons of the hand and arm joints. These fine tremors stimulate relays which create motor memories reflecting the movements (and subsequent shapes) which are being created. Rollerballs and biros cause less vibration and therefore have a reduced effect on motor learning and the subsequent memory of letter shapes. Some schools have introduced mini-whiteboards to aid spelling and letter production. Again, these do not provide the kinaesthetic feedback that writing with pencil on paper (or chalk on a blackboard) affords.

Another benefit of using a pencil is how it responds to pressure. Even the lightest touch can leave a mark and therefore it is a useful monitor by which children can experiment with and learn to adjust the force they exert when writing through the pencil point. Such adjustment is not possible when using a pen.

The average pencil can withstand a pressure of nearly 1701kg before breaking!

A further reason for learning to write using a pencil is that they are the least expensive writing tool and do not run out; they simply need to be sharpened. They are also leak-proof and more robust when handled by little hands.

Once a child has mastered the initial stages of handwriting, the effort required to write can be diverted to stimulate higher-order cognitive demands such as spelling and composition. At this stage, speed of output is more important and the child can transition to using a pen.

Unfortunately, the classroom incentive of allowing a child to write in pen when they have achieved effective neat handwriting in pencil can have a negative effect on those who struggle to master this complex skill, making early dents to their fragile self-esteem and confidence. This is particularly true for children who have motor co-ordination difficulties such as developmental co-ordination disorder (DCD).

> *My child's school issues pen licences when [pupils'] writing is consistently neat and tidy. My child has severe dyspraxia, and left school at the end of Year 6 having never got his pen licence. It was very demoralising.*
> Member of Mumsnet, 2013

Any writing tool is only as effective as the individual who is manipulating it, and therefore the importance of adopting an effective grip has been stressed repeatedly in handwriting research (Selin, 2003; Soechting & Flanders, 2008; Falk et al., 2010). When considering what an effective or abnormal grip is, a general rule should be applied: if the pencil or pen grip is atypical, yet the writing being produced is legible and neat, with adequate pressure, speed and output, and if the writer does not appear to be uncomfortable or complain of aches or pains in the hand or wrist, then the grip (however unusual it may appear) should be left alone. However, if the written output appears slow and laboured, if the individual looks uncomfortable or complains of aches, pains or sweaty palms, or becomes hesitant or reluctant to write, then an alternative position needs to be sought.

In order for a pencil grip to be functional, the user must be able to produce legible script for a required duration. Children need to be able to keep up with their classwork, so it is important that when we consider the part that pencil grip plays on the writing process, we also consider writing stamina. Research has found that children who adopt certain pencil grips other than the dynamic tripod grip (see below) can initially produce legible writing but cannot sustain this for an extended period. As they tire, so the legibility of their writing deteriorates (Stevens, 2008).

It is interesting that in the UK, most of our GCSE and A level examinations require young people to write their answers under exam conditions over periods of between 1–2 hours. However, the assessments used to determine exam accommodations (i.e. access arrangements) do not evaluate writing produced over this timeframe, so a true understanding of the link between grip, writing legibility and fatigue is often not identified.

The ideal writing grip has been referred to as the **dynamic tripod grip** (Figure 24). This grip demands that the thumb and index finger create a triangle with the middle finger, hence the term *tripod*. This grip allows the pencil to be finely controlled by the fingers rather than the wrist. It allows the pencil to touch the paper at a diagonal so the writer can observe the marks being made and adjust pressure through the fingers, which are placed approximately 2cm from the pencil point. This is classed as a mature grip and is functional due to the activation of the intrinsic muscles of the hand (these are shorter muscles responsible for minute alterations to the position of the fingers), in comparison to immature grips which are reliant on the movements of the extrinsic muscles (Schwellnus et al., 2013). The dynamic tripod grip facilitates smooth, fluid strokes, with the ring and fifth finger providing stability through contact with the paper (Ziviani & Wallen, 2006). However, the focus on encouraging a dynamic tripod grip has been challenged in more recent years, possibly due to the change in the way we use our hands in response to new technology. For example, our thumbs have developed in responsiveness and proficiency to texting and gaming with increasing speed and spontaneity (Schwellnus et al., 2013).

Figure 24: Dynamic tripod grip

Occasionally, children will adopt a grip which slightly deviates from this and position the thumb joint over the shaft of the pencil. Pencil control continues to come from the thumb and index finger, but this is a slightly less fluent position. This is known as the **lateral tripod grip** (Figure 25). Although this position prevents the writer from seeing their index finger and pressure can appear quite heavy, it can still be very effective.

Figure 25: Lateral tripod grip

This grip in particular reflects advances in technology and subsequent changes in motor control. Only a decade ago, children played with construction toys and creative activities such as Lego™, Meccano®, K'NEX®, Scalextric®, dressing dolls and craft tasks. Today, although these games remain popular, the majority of young children are increasingly familiar with and proficient in the use of interactive computer games involving hand-held operating controls which demand rapid thumb and index finger reactions. This is influencing children's dexterity, and therefore we must accept some positional changes in the use of the writing tool as a result.

Although the lateral tripod grip is a tight grip and can limit the pencil's movement due to the restricted movement of the thumb, it can be functionally effective (Schwellnus et al. 2013). However, for some, this will put some strain on the finger joints and prevent the writer from seeing the pencil point without sitting at an angle. Therefore careful observation is needed to monitor whether this is a functionally-effective grip over a prolonged period of time, especially as children using this grip may press down harder than usual and writing may be slower and heavier (although still precise). Research has found that children and young people who adopt this grip tend to stop writing sooner into a task due to fatigue (Stevens, 2008).

The **dynamic quadrupod grip** (Figure 26) brings the thumb, index, middle and ring finger (four digits, hence the term *quad*) in contact with the barrel of the pencil, which may lose some stability due to the way the ring and fifth fingers are in contact with the writing surface. However, the force exerted through the pencil point can be controlled reasonably well.

Figure 26: Dynamic quadrupod grip

The **lateral quadrupod grip** (Figure 27) is another grip which allows the thumb to roll over the barrel of the pencil while keeping four digits in contact with the pencil. This grip rests the pencil in the thumb web space to secure its position. Again, this is a tight but stable grip which is controlled by the index and middle fingers. The disadvantage of this is the limited manipulation of the thumb, making the effort of writing the responsibility of the index finger.

Figure 27: Lateral quadrupod grip

Some pencil grips are less productive, mature or functional. We have previously referred to the left-handed hooked position (Figure 22) which allows the writer to see what they are writing but at the expense of pressure on the wrist. Another is the **inverted abducted grip** (Figure 28), where the hand is inverted and fingers spread and then flexed so that the fingertips are touching the shaft of the pencil, and the pencil points towards the writer and is pushed towards the body to effect script. This grip allows left-handed writers to see what they are writing but will cause the wrist and fingers to cramp and spasm. Therefore this is not a good long-term position to adopt and should be altered.

Figure 28: Inverted abducted grip

Other immature grips involve a fisted position or one where the fingers weave around the pencil. When considering these unusual grips, it is important to consider why they are being used; understanding is paramount to determining a solution. Some of the potential reasons why children and young people adopt these unusual grips are listed below.

Poor fine motor co-ordination

Good fine motor control is essential for producing legible handwriting. If an individual experiences difficulties in this area, they will need to be introduced to activities which build fine motor skills. In-hand manipulation games and other fine motor activities can serve to enhance the dexterity required for handwriting, and these can be included before and after handwriting lessons. These can include tweezer games and other activities (see Appendix C for further ideas).

Reduced tactile sensation

Some children have reduced tactile sensation. This may be due to neurological differences, injury or specific circumstances that have affected sensation (e.g. children with brittle diabetes may have limited tactile sensation due to the regular pin pricks that they have to administer in order to determine blood sugar levels). These individuals may adopt heavier grips in order to stimulate a larger surface area of the skin to obtain the feedback that is missing from the fingertips. This can be helped by using pencil grips which are heavily textured and therefore provide additional input as to where to locate the fingers on the pen(cil).

Low muscle tone (hypomobile joints)

Children and young people with low muscle tone may also adopt a tighter pen(cil) grip as they do not receive the same tactile feedback as others and therefore crave this input by adopting a very tight grip, which in turn affects pressure and control. This can be improved to some extent by muscle-strengthening activities such as squeezing clay into shapes, rolling pastry or dough or painting using a pipette bulb and paint. Although the long-term effects of these grip-strengthening activities may be limited, the proprioceptive feedback obtained through the games can enhance a child's awareness of their fingers and their subsequent positioning (Celletti et al., 2011; Palmer et al., 2014).

Joint pain caused by juvenile arthritis or other rheumatology complaints will also affect an individual's grip on a pen(cil). The manipulation involved in writing puts a considerable strain on many of the smaller joints in the hand. This can cause children to adapt their grip in order to reduce pain. These individuals may need the support of an ergonomic writing support such as the Writing Bird (Figure 40) to help them throughout these painful periods, or the use of technology as an adjunct to handwriting.

Alternative grip and ergonomic writing tools

An alternative to an abnormal or unproductive grip is to position the pen(cil) in a **prone grip** (Figure 29). This positions the hand palm down, with the pencil held between the index and middle finger. The control comes from the thumb and index finger, and the wrist is supported on the writing surface. It is a useful alternative for both left- and right-handers. It is a particularly useful grip for writers who have cerebral palsy, who may struggle to **supinate** their hand (i.e. turn or hold it so the palm is facing upwards) to hold a pencil in a lateral position. It is also an excellent alternative for those who have juvenile rheumatoid arthritis as it applies less pressure on the finger joints.

Figure 29: Prone grip

Another way to encourage an effective pen(cil) grip is to provide the writer with an ergonomically-designed pencil or pen which repositions the writing tool within the writer's hand. We are all unique in our approach to handwriting and, indeed, our manipulation of the writing instrument. Therefore, it is important to understand that one tool is not going to meet the needs of all writers. A range of tools should be provided for children and young people to experiment with in order to find their own level of comfort. Unfortunately, some ergonomically-designed tools are only available as pens rather than pencils, due to their shape. The following are a selection of tools which have been found to be very effective in supporting individuals with handwriting difficulties.

The **Yoropen** (Figure 30) is one of the few ergonomically-designed writing instruments available in pen, pencil and crayon. The position of the nib opens up the space between the fingers and the paper, enabling the child to see what they are writing. The rubber positioning grip can be rotated for the comfort of both left- and right-handers. The offset position of the nib makes it impossible to hold too near to the writing surface. This device looks unusual but is very effective for both left- and right-handers.

Figure 30: Yoropen

Figure 31: PenAgain

The **PenAgain** (Figure 31) is also available as a pencil or pen. It has a unique wishbone shape, which encourages the correct positioning of the index finger, making control of the writing instrument easier. Once again, the shape restricts the writer's ability to hold the device too near to the point. Children often call this the 'rocket pen' due to its shape, and as a consequence it is seen as being cool, particularly by boys who struggle to control a traditional pen(cil).

The tiny 6cm-long **EVO Pen** (Figure 32) fits snugly into the small palm of a child's hand. Its size and shape restricts awkward thumb rotation and demands a dynamic tripod grip to operate it effectively. It allows the hand to rest on the table or writing slope, offering stability when writing. It does not accommodate lead due to its size, so can only be bought as a biro.

Figure 32: EVO Pen

The **EZ Grip Pen** (Figure 33) is a relatively heavy pen and has a sculptured design which locates the thumb and fingers appropriately on a rubber positioning grip. It requires very little pressure and encourages a dynamic tripod grip. The heaviness of the pen provides additional downward pressure, helping those who struggle to apply the right amount of force through the writing tool. The grip itself is quite broad but comfortable. The ink flows freely and writing occurs with the pen held at most angles, whether an individual is left- or right-handed.

Figure 33: EZ Grip Pen

The **Ring Pen** (Figure 34) is an ergonomically-designed pen that places the index finger through a ring in order to align it exactly to the pen shaft. There is a textured pad which helps to locate the end of the finger. It is possible to still roll the thumb using this device but the position of the index finger improves control significantly. This device is particularly useful for those who seem to constantly alter their finger position when writing, or for those who seem to drop their pen(cil) easily.

Figure 34: Ring Pen

The **Ring Pen Ultra** (Figure 35) is a slightly different version of the Ring Pen and places the pen(cil) in a more lateral position, enabling the writer to see the pen(cil) nib more easily. The advantage of this gripper is that it can accommodate the individual's own pen or pencil.

Figure 35: Ring Pen Ultra

Stabilo make an excellent range of ergonomically-adaptable pens, crayons, fibretips and pencils. The **S Move** (Figure 36) fits nicely into the contours of the hand to encourage an effective dynamic tripod grip and is available in left- and right-handed versions. The **Basketball Pen** (Figure 37) is a straighter fineliner, but its non-slip surface encourages the fingers to remain in an accurately placed position. This is more suited to those who do not exert too much force through the pen point.

Figure 36: S Move Pen

There are a number of pens which have a triangular shaft. These actively encourage the writer to adopt a dynamic tripod grip. These include the Pelikan Twist® rollerball and fountain pen, Nexus Handwriter, Bic Tri-Stic Pen, and Berol Hand Huggers, to name but a few.

Figure 37: Basketball Pen

In addition to ergonomically-designed pen(cil)s, there is also a range of rubber grips which can be added to the shaft of the pencil to encourage the accurate placement of the fingers.

Noodle Doodle grips (Figure 38) are long tacky grips which can be stretched to cover the length of a pen(cil) or scrunched up to fit just where you want to grip. A cheaper alternative (though not so visually aesthetic), is to place rubber bands or Loom Bands approximately 3cm from the pencil point.

Figure 38: Noodle Doodle grips

The **HandiWriter**® (Figure 39) is a simple but clever device which helps the child to learn where to locate the fingers when writing. It consists of two soft elastic loops with an attached charm on a short string. It particularly helps to tuck the ring and little fingers away by encouraging the child to grip onto an attached charm, enabling the other fingers to focus on the correct position on the pen(cil). The charms vary, with options including a dolphin, football and baseball.

Figure 39: HandiWriter

There are a range of smaller grips which can be added to the pen(cil) to encourage a more dynamic writing grip. It is best to experiment with these to identify which will prove more comfortable for the individual. Some of these smaller grips are noted below:

- The **Crossover**, which has been described as the pencil grip with wings! It holds the thumb and index finger securely, establishing a dynamic tripod writing position and preventing thumb and index finger from crossing over. It is impossible to roll the thumb or index finger.
- The **Solo** looks like a sting ray and encourages the same position as the Crossover, yet is smaller and more compact for little hands. It goes on pencils the same way for left- and right-handed users. The *R* and *L* indicate the correct thumb placement, and index and middle fingers then fall comfortably into place.
- The **Ultra Pencil Grip** is larger and therefore provides a comprehensive grip on the pencil for older children in particular. The position of the fingers is clearly located, and its soft plastic provides support for those who have low muscle tone or 'floppy' fingers. This is available in both left- and right-handed versions.
- The **Triangle** is the most common attachment and familiar to many. It provides a simple way of forming a dynamic tripod grip, although it does not prevent the crossover of the thumb and index finger. It can be attached to most pens and pencils.
- The **EZ Grip** helps to localise the index finger appropriately on the pencil so that it exerts pressure downwards through the pen(cil). This grip fits most standard pencils and crayons.

When children and young people either struggle to apply an appropriate amount of force through their pen(cil) or have a lack of upper limb strength, a specialised desk-based writing support will help. These are resources which rest on the writing page and limit the amount of pressure placed through the pen(cil) point, allowing the writer to focus on letter formation, writing legibility and content.

The **Writing Bird** is one of these supports. It is a perspex 'mouse', which can hold a pen(cil) secured using a screw (Figure 40). Writing is achieved by manoeuvring the Writing Bird in the same way as a computer mouse. Its shape and qualities allow it to glide across the paper. The Writing Bird is useful for those who cannot control the force of pressure through the writing tool, for those who have juvenile arthritis which means that a usual pencil grip is too painful on their joints, and for those with muscle weakness seen in conditions such as muscular dystrophy. The Writing Bird requires very little effort to use and requires no grip strength. It can be used for those who are left- or right-handed.

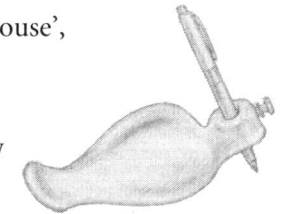

Figure 40: Writing Bird

The **Steady Write Grip** (Figure 41) offers similar support, and younger children may enjoy writing using the funky **Giotto Be-Be Egg** (Figure 42) which looks and operates exactly like a handwriting computer mouse.

Figure 41: Steady Write Grip

Figure 42: Giotto Be-Be Egg

A further support for children and young people who experience joint pain or who have restricted movements in their fingers is the **ball grip** (Figure 43). This is a plastic or rubber ball with an adjustable core that can hold a pen(cil). Gripping the ball places less stress on the finger joints and alleviates pain for those who have juvenile arthritis and other musculoskeletal impairments. There are various brands of this type of grip available, such as the Arthwriter®, Abilitations Egg Ohs! or Writing Grip Helper. A cheaper alternative is to simply place a pen(cil) through a tennis ball or sponge ball.

Figure 43: Ball grip

Summary

Research has demonstrated the importance of handedness and pen(cil) grip on the successful production of legible handwriting (Rosenblum et al., 2006; Schewllnus et al., 2014; Bebey, 2014). For example, we know that children who struggle to acquire an accurate pencil grip have been found to make more alterations to their grip when writing, slowing the process down and reducing output. This chapter has focused on these facets and has suggested how we can determine an individual's handedness and encourage an effective grip on the pencil, crayon or pen through positioning or the use of an ergonomic writing tool.

The importance of developing fine motor co-ordination and in-hand manipulation skills in preparation for writing has also been highlighted, encouraging educators to introduce activities which promote dexterity before any formal handwriting tuition (Ohl et al., 2013; Visser et al., 2014; Lifshitz & Har-Zvi, 2015).

CHAPTER 4
A process-orientated approach to handwriting

In order to write effectively, there are a number of foundation skills that need to be in place. These are developmentally-appropriate sensory, perceptual and physical skills that provide the building blocks from which higher order skills can emerge. They include dexterity, an appreciation of form, visual-spatial organisation and visual-motor integration. Sometimes these skills are not evident in a child before they are introduced to the complexities of handwriting, causing them to fail in their early attempts to form letters with a negative impact on their self-esteem and enjoyment of the task. This is an issue of particular concern for boys (Beard & Burrell, 2010).

The human brain is malleable (or *plastic*) and responds to instructions from childhood right through to adulthood. During this time there are specific critical periods associated with key periods of development when the brain is particularly receptive to change owing to surges in hormones, such as periods of growth in early childhood and during puberty. These times could be seen as 'windows of opportunity' for new skills to be learned.

The development of the perceptual, kinaesthetic and motor components of handwriting which are so crucial to the effective production of legible writing can be acquired through playful activities during the early years, and later in a more targeted form in Readiness to Write programmes. Although controversial, there is an argument for targeting perceptual-motor and kinaesthetic facets of handwriting during the early years. This is also considered appropriate for those with specific difficulties in perceptual-motor processing (i.e. those with developmental co-ordination disorder (DCD) or dysgraphia) (Sajedi & Barati, 2014; Dinehart, 2014). The controversy around this argument has two premises:

1 Whether or not it is possible to improve or enhance perceptual-motor skills.
2 Whether or not that by improving perceptual-motor aspects of handwriting, other activities requiring effective perceptual-motor organisation can also be improved. (For example, if a child struggles to leave adequate spaces between words, targeting their spatial planning ability will not only help to improve their writing organisation, but also help them in other activities requiring spatial planning, such as dodgeball and co-ordinating around the classroom.)

It is therefore worthwhile considering how these processes could be enhanced and whether there is any evidence to suggest this is possible.

The targeting of the underlying dysfunctional process skills required for handwriting adopts a process-orientated (or bottom-up) approach. This contrasts with the task-specific (or top-down) approach which will be described in the next chapter. In handwriting, there are three process-orientated approaches that are often used (although many teachers and therapists adopt an eclectic mix of all three methods); one which focuses on the **perceptual-motor** aspects of handwriting, one which focuses on the **sensory-motor** facets of writing, and another which addresses the **kinaesthetic** qualities of handwriting, incorporating aspects of **motor imagery**. These are examined in more detail below.

Perceptual-motor approach to handwriting

It is important to consider the perceptual-motor components of handwriting and explore how these can be enhanced in order to encourage the production of legible handwriting. The perceptual-motor writing programme *Write from the Start* (Teodorescu & Addy, 1996) adopts this approach. This chapter includes examples taken from the programme.

Perceptual-motor components of handwriting include:

1. In-hand manipulation
2. Hand–eye co-ordination (or visual-motor integration)
3. Perception of form (including size and shape)
4. Orientation
5. Figure-ground discrimination
6. Spatial relationships and spatial organisation
7. Visual closure (based on Gestalt psychology)

In-hand manipulation

In-hand manipulation activities predominantly help with the subtle adjustment of pen(cil) positioning during the writing process. This links to the importance of adopting an effective grip on the pen(cil) in order to respond to the intricate muscle requirements involved in producing script.

> *In-hand manipulation is the process of using one hand to adjust an object for more effective object placement, or release; the object remains in that hand and does not usually come into contact with a surface during the process.*
> Exner, 1997

There is evidence of a positive relationship between in-hand manipulation and handwriting, with in-hand manipulation being a vital precursor to pen(cil) control and subsequent hand–eye co-ordination (Cornhill & Case-Smith, 1996; Exner, 2005; Pont et al., 2008; Bazyk et al., 2009).

In-hand manipulation involves three primary movements: **shift**, **translation** and **rotation** (Exner, 1989). Shift involves moving an object between the fingers, translation involves moving an object from the palm of the hand to the tips of the fingers, and rotation is the ability to turn the object 360º in the hand in a 'windmill' motion. In-hand manipulation activities can involve turning pegs on a pegboard, rotating coins in the hand, and 'walking' the fingers up the barrel of a pencil. See Appendix C for further examples.

There is support for introducing in-hand manipulation activities during the early years as these activities can positively enhance early pencil control (e.g. the ability to form letters), together with other fine motor activities such as bead threading, placing pegs and other functional skills such as fastening buttons (Wehrmann et al., 2006; Bazyk et al., 2009).

Stages of in-hand manipulation	
0–6 months	No in-hand manipulation
12–15 months	Finger–palm translation emerges
2–3 years	Can manipulate object in one hand, stabilising with the other
3–4 years	Complex rotation develops
3–5 years	Most children can shift, rotate and translate
6+ years	In-hand manipulation with stabilisation occurs

(Visser et al., 2014)

Hand–eye co-ordination (visual-motor integration)

These terms are interchangeable and describe the ability of the eyes and hands to work together in a smooth, efficient manner. Hand–eye co-ordination is the ability to integrate visual input with motor output and involves the co-ordination of two independent functions: visual perception and fine motor control. It enables individuals to plan, act and monitor motor tasks, such as threading a needle, tying shoe laces and catching or hitting a ball. It is essential to all aspects of learning and a vital component of handwriting. It helps to develop skills in motor accuracy and psychomotor speed (i.e. how fast something is copied, written or manipulated). In writing, it helps with tracking and letter orientation.

Sometimes we expect children to write before basic hand–eye co-ordination is in place. There are children who are unable to co-ordinate the movements of their hands with what they are seeing. This may be evident in their inability to stack cube bricks on top of each other without them toppling over, or to place a pencil at the appropriate spot to start to write a letter. These children may have adequate vision and adequate fine motor skills, but struggle to integrate or combine these two systems together. This is evident in many children born prematurely and those with DCD (Cantin et al., 2014; Pinheiro et al., 2014).

When children have difficulties in visual-motor integration they will struggle to produce the basic shapes required to write effectively. However, there are some strategies and activities that can be implemented to improve this integration.

Firstly, it is important to determine whether the difficulties in hand–eye co-ordination are due to a visual impairment, rather than a visual perceptual difficulty. If the child repeatedly places objects to one side of where they should be, they could have a **nystagmus** (involuntary eye movement), **strabismus** (squint) or a **hemianopia** (decreased vision in half of the visual field). These require the expertise of an optician or ophthalmologist, and the provision of corrective lenses.

Once potential issues around vision are ruled out, it is important to observe the child undertaking a fine motor task, noting their seating position and trunk control. This will help to evaluate whether the individual is struggling to place objects accurately due to poor postural (core) stability. If this is the case, activities to enhance postural stability should be provided (see Appendices A and B).

An inability to place objects accurately may also be due to poor regulation of pressure through the limbs (proprioception). If this is the case, the pelvic and shoulder girdle stability activities in

Appendices A and B will also help. Activities which teach the self-regulation of pressure referred to in Chapter 2 (e.g. using light-up pens) can also be used.

Finally, activities to assist visual-motor integration can be introduced throughout the day. These may include tracking exercises or mazes which progressively increase in complexity, *Join the dots* games, origami, scissor skills activities, bead threading, geoboards, and copying pegboard patterns. Older children can also benefit from model-making, pottery, woodwork and other practical tasks, together with physical games such as swing ball and badminton. These can be altered to accommodate the speed of the individual's visuomotor processing (Cho et al., 2015; Brown & Link, 2015).

Games will need to be carefully graded, starting from activities that are relatively easy to those that demand more visual effort. For example, *Spot the difference* involves careful observation of two pictures and circling the different parts in one of the images; these can become increasingly complicated in order to extend the individual's visual focus. Some physical games can be adapted to slow down the visual-motor process to give more time to those who are struggling to process the information. For example, volleyball is an excellent visual-motor activity; however, the ball is passed backward and forward over the net at considerable speed. To slow this down, a balloon could be used to allow players time to co-ordinate hand and eye movements.

There are mixed opinions as to whether the introduction of visual-motor integration activities can have an influence on improving handwriting legibility. Ratzon et al. (2009) showed significant gains on tests of hand–eye co-ordination after specific input was provided in this area compared to a control group. Bara et al. (2011) found that activities such as those described above improved hand–eye co-ordination per se as well as an understanding of form, whereas Poon et al. (2010) found that they could help to make improvements to handwriting speed but not legibility. The latter study supported specific practice of creating the forms or shapes essential for writing.

Perception of form

The lines and shapes required to write in English are limited to the combination of approximately five strokes and therefore children must be able to reproduce these in order to write the letters of the English alphabet. These strokes are:

— | ○ + ✕

Feder & Majnemer (2007) suggested that children must learn these basic strokes in various directions before they create more precise shapes and, subsequently, letters and numbers. They suggest that there is an approximate developmental framework:

2 years	Can imitate geometric shapes, commencing with vertical strokes
2.6 years	Can draw horizontal strokes
3 years	Can draw circles
4 years	Can copy a cross
5 years	Can draw a square
5.6 years	Can draw a triangle

They recommend that when a child is able to copy geometric forms, particularly the oblique cross, the child is considered to be ready to write.

The ability to understand and appreciate these shapes is the basis of visual form constancy. This also helps the individual to recognise an object or shape when presented from a number of angles or dimensions. The appreciation of form is gained through experience and experimentation. For example, by touching, seeing and playing with a ball, a child begins to appreciate a round shape. Some children struggle to develop this skill due to poor feedback through their motor, tactile and visual systems and therefore need more input and practice to embed their understanding of form.

Initially, it is important that children practise the simple shape. In the following example taken from *Write from the Start* (Teodorescu & Addy, 1996), the writer is encouraged to create circles in both anti-clockwise and clockwise direction, using the finely highlighted dots for guidance (Figure 44). This can be supplemented with other sensory-motor activities such as drawing circles on the pavement with chalk (Figure 45), creating circles out of dough and drawing circles in sand.

Figure 44: Orientation practice (*Write from the Start*, Book 1, Booklet 1C, page 7)

Figure 45: Creating forms to produce letters

Once a clear circle has been established, it is important to determine whether this is constant (i.e. whether the individual has a clear motor and visual understanding of that shape). Challenge them to draw a circle within another shape. If the form is fully embedded, the individual will be able to distinguish between the two shapes. If the form is not constant, the child will become visually distracted by the previous shape and will produce an unclear form, suggesting that they need further help in establishing the difference between shapes before they can progress in handwriting. If this is not addressed, the child will become visually attracted to previous letter shapes when they write and their writing will appear distorted (Figure 46).

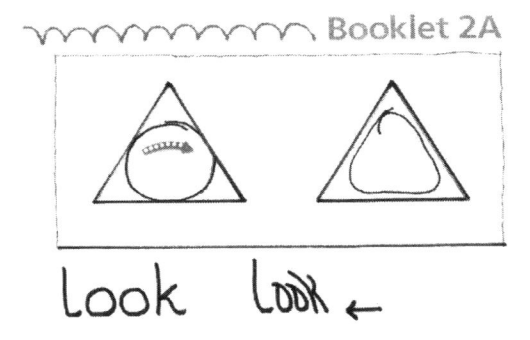

Figure 46: Distortions in letter shapes as a consequence of poor visual form constancy

Orientation

Orientation describes the position of an object in space. It is a perceptual phenomenon which affects handwriting by determining the orientation of the letter. Difficulties in appreciating position in space can result in letter inversions and reversals, often seen in confusions of the production of *p/b*, *d/b*, *f/t*, *w/m*, *n/u* and *p/q*. In extreme cases, children can write in mirror form, so that writing can only be read if you look in a mirror. It is often thought that this is a problem which is particularly evident in those who are left-handed, but research disputes this (Cubelli & Salla, 2009; Fischer & Tazouti, 2012).

Difficulties in appreciating position in space can affect movement around objects, an appreciation of left and right and an understanding of spatial concepts and following directions, and can also impact on an individual's ability to learn to drive, with parking being particularly problematic (De Oliveira & Wann, 2012).

It is possible to improve skills in this area using spatial organisation games and activities such as identifying inverted items, spatial copying activities using pegboards and geoboards, mental rotation tasks, and pattern blocks and boards challenges (Figure 47). Games can also be used to identify direction (e.g. mazes), while apps and computer games (such as SEMERC's Letter Olympics), and Wii Fit™ activities can serve to develop orientation, as can gross motor activities such as *Port/Starboard*, obstacle courses and orienteering (Ehrlich et al., 2006).

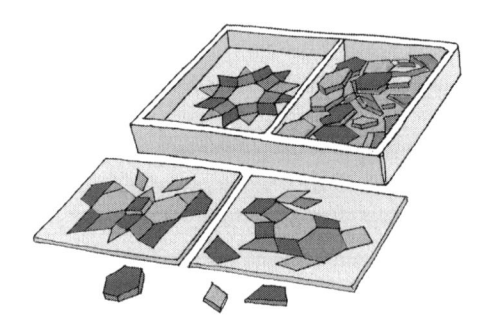

Figure 47: Pattern blocks and boards

While games are motivating, there is a need to overtly practise the orientation of letters and see how these fit together to create a word. The motor processes involved in producing the desired letter shapes contribute to the visual recognition of letters. Interestingly, Longcamp (2006) found that when letter characters had been learned through typing, they were more frequently confused with their mirror images than when they had been written by hand. In addition, Fischer (2010 & 2011) found that left-facing letters such as *j*, *d*, *q* and *z* were confused more than right-facing letters. Research has suggested that this left-right confusion depends on linguistic skills (where many children demonstrate phoneme association difficulties), and up-down confusions such as *p/d* and *f/t* are linked to perceptual factors such as directional or visuospatial organisation (Uehara, 2013).

Figure-ground discrimination

Figure-ground discrimination is the ability to visually separate a figure (key object) from its background. It helps to organise and filter the volume of visual images in a given environment. This is an important aspect of visual attention. When writing, poor figure-ground discrimination can be responsible for page organisation issues. This will cause children to be unsure of where to start their writing, and writing may commence away from the margin, or follow a downward direction. The writer may alternatively be visually distracted by the previous line of script and veer towards this (Figure 48).

Figure 48: This child's writing veers towards the initial line

To prevent this happening, it is important to encourage children to write on lined paper (rather than using line guides or plain paper). This helps them learn where to place their letters and the margin provides their starting position. Some writers may need a more overt reference and may require raised line paper, which provides a kinaesthetic prompt and guides the writing across the page from left to right.

Paper which has a line reference above (for ascending letters) and below (for descending letters) can also assist with spatial planning and the appropriate sizing of letters. Lines can be coloured as on Ground, Grass and Sky Paper, where the descending line is brown (ground), the central line is green (grass) and the ascending line is blue (sky).

Further figure-ground discrimination activities can be added into sessions which focus on handwriting to engage the child or young person whilst helping to focus their attention. These can include S*pot the difference* puzzles, *Where's Wally?* books and posters and Usborne's puzzle books (e.g. *Puzzle Castle*).

Spatial relationships and spatial organisation

Handwriting is fundamentally a visuospatial activity. Visual-spatial integration refers to processing visual information so that an individual can move around in an environment, orientate appropriately, accurately reach for objects, understand visual patterns and shift gaze to different points in space. When writing, it can make the difference as to whether text is legible or not. To demonstrate this, try to read the following texts where 1) spaces have been omitted between words, and 2) spaces have been inserted incorrectly.

1

Comeletusstrayourgladsomewayandviewthecharmsofnaturetherustlingcornthefruitedthornandeveryhappycreature

2

Therewa sa ayoun gmanfr omGo ffamwhotoo kout hiseyeba llstowashemhi smothersaidjackif youdontput them backl 'llstandon thoseeye balls andsq uashthem

To improve spatial planning, children could be introduced to cursive writing during their early years. They must be able to see how the letters they produce connect to create words, otherwise they are simply drawing. Encouraging cursive handwriting from the beginning can show children where the spaces should be and subsequently improve legibility.

Specific activities which target spatial planning can be particularly helpful in improving the spaces a child leaves between words. These can be incorporated into Readiness to Write programmes and other class-based lessons. They can include tracking mazes, following Lego™ instructions, copying a picture, following maps, computer games and jigsaw puzzles, and manoeuvring around obstacle courses.

Pencil and paper tracking activities can also be included, such as those seen in Figure 49, which requires the individual to jump over and under the spines on the dragons' backs. Tracking activities should increase in complexity.

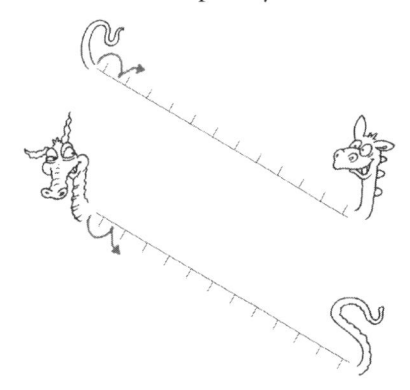

Figure 49: Pencil and paper tracking practice (*Write from the Start*, Book 1, Booklet 2B, page 7)

The question of whether or not spatial relationships can be improved with training and practice was answered in part by Uttal et al. (2013), who analysed 206 spatial training studies and found an improvement which lasted over time and could also be generalised to other tasks. Several of these interventions involved the analysis of video gaming on improving visuospatial integration, with positive results.

Visual closure

Visual closure is the ability to see a part of an object and predict what it looks like as a whole unit. It is part of Gestalt psychology, a school of thought which helps us to understand perception. The Gestalt Law of Closure explains how we naturally group visual information together in order to obtain a whole image. In other words, our brains see a whole image and then latterly fill in gaps in information. For example, when we look at a tree, we initially look at it in its entirety to appreciate what it is. We can then determine its structure by focusing on detail such as twigs, leaves, buds and bark. This ability is often different in children and young people with autism, who will often focus on the parts of an object rather than its whole. This can be very confusing, especially when the parts being observed appear to constantly change (e.g. when looking at someone's face).

When applied to writing, children and young people who have difficulties with visual closure will struggle to see the connectedness of letter shapes. For example, they might see the letter *a* as a circle and a stick rather than the letter as a whole. They may be unable to appreciate the connectedness of letters when these are grouped together to create a word (Figure 50). Again, this difficulty can be alleviated by teaching cursive handwriting as this provides the missing connections between letter shapes, helping children and young people to 'see' the word as a whole.

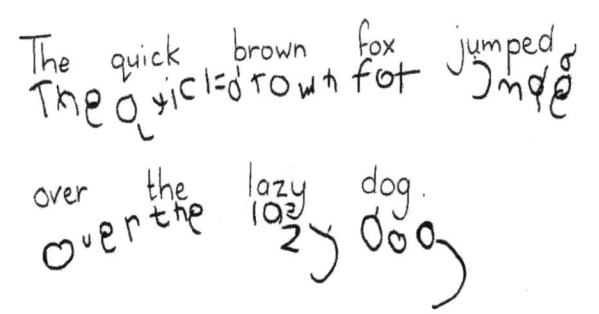

Figure 50: Sample of handwriting from a child who has difficulties with visual closure

Activities which help children see the connectedness in images can help to reduce the effects of visual closure difficulties. These include completing drawings where part is missing (Figure 51), jigsaw puzzles which get progressively more complex, completing a mirror image of an object where only half is given, and guessing what an object is when only a small part is seen.

Figure 51: Visual closure practice (*Write from the Start*, Book 1, Booklet 3C, page 25)

Critique of the perceptual-motor approach

The perceptual-motor approach to addressing handwriting difficulties has been criticised for its focus on 'splinter skills' connected to handwriting, rather than targeting the handwriting product itself. However, evidence shows that targeted input can help children who do not have clearly-established visual perceptual skills. Therefore, it is acceptable to suggest that perceptual-motor activities could be incorporated into Readiness to Write programmes so that direct practice of letter formation can be supplemented by perceptual-motor activities. *Write from the Start*, for example, was never intended to be used in isolation but instead in parallel with activities which focus on letter formation. The results gained from using such an approach can be visually significant (Figure 52).

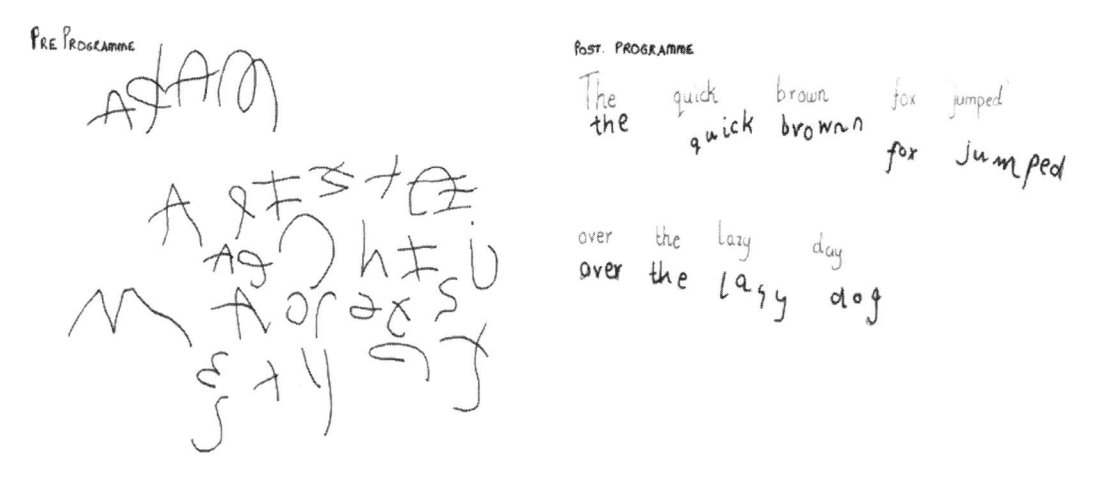

Figure 52: Handwriting samples from a child with DCD, aged 5.8, before and after using the *Write from the Start* programme

Research has suggested that pockets of learning opportunity can arise at around the age of 4–6 years old, but particular changes in visuomotor integration and visuospatial perception can be observed between 6–7 years of age (Terebova & Bezrukikh, 2009). This approach is predominantly recommended for these age groups.

Sensory-motor approach to handwriting

A similar method of teaching handwriting is the use of sensorimotor or multi-sensory strategies. This approach does not systematically address perceptual components such as those identified in the perceptual-motor approach. Rather, it uses a range of mark-making activities which stimulate the whole body's sensory and motor systems to learn to write.

It adopts an approach that feels natural to teaching children during the early years as it is play-based and motivational. It incorporates the whole body in appreciating the forms required to write and uses various methods for reinforcing size, shape and position.

Write Dance (Oussoren, 2010) is one handwriting intervention which adopts this approach. It uses whole body movements and music to teach children about the rhythm required in handwriting, and variations in the size and shape of various letters. It encourages wrist flexibility, speed and direction of movement. It introduces children to 'scrimbling', which is the use of one- and two-handed multi-sensory doodling activities which involve chalk, paint, sand and crayon. Stories are included to guide children's movements and so it is engaging and motivating, while boosting the practice of rhythmic motor patterning in readiness for writing. This programme encourages children to develop shoulder girdle stability and kinaesthetic motor patterns in preparation for formal handwriting.

There is little objective evidence regarding the effectiveness of this programme. However, there are many examples from schools describing the motivational qualities of the programme and how it encourages the rhythm and motor control required to write effectively. Owen (2009) studied teachers' perceptions of this programme and found that, when used alongside other handwriting activities, teachers believed that children's fine motor control improved. Teachers also reported benefits to children's self-esteem, which in turn gave them the freedom to experiment in mark-making without the fear of failure.

Further multi-sensory handwriting programmes include the *Callirobics* series (Laufer, 1991). This utilises music, rhythm and writing patterns, and focuses more on fine motor skills than whole-body movements. *TRICS for Written Communication* (Amundson, 1998) and *Handwriting Without Tears* (Olsen, 2001) are also multi-sensory courses designed to teach students with varied learning styles using visual, auditory, manipulative, tactile and kinaesthetic methods. According to Olsen, the *Handwriting Without Tears* programme may help to 'eliminate problems with letter formation, reversals, legibility, sentence spacing, and cursive connections'. Improvements in the area of letter size and spacing have been found to be evident following the use of this intervention (Hape et al., 2014).

Critique of the sensory-motor approach

The adoption of a multi-sensory approach to handwriting does not improve handwriting legibility directly. However, it does enhance the foundation skills required for children to write, in particular motor skills (Chia & Chua, 2002; Wilson et al., 2002). The key attributes of the approach are the motivational qualities of the programmes and the inclusion of activities which promote core stability, fine and gross motor control, rhythm and perceptual readiness in anticipation of formal handwriting tuition.

Kinaesthetic approach to handwriting

Handwriting interventions which focus on enhancing the kinaesthetic sense in relation to writing also come under the umbrella of a process-orientated (or bottom-up) approach. This approach is concerned with developing the kinaesthetic representations of the handwriting process through the use of movement and/or proprioceptive feedback, without a dependence on vision. Proprioception is the awareness of the limbs' position and, according to Laszlo (1991), is virtually the most important aspect of perceptual development. When handwriting, proprioception provides feedback as to the position of the hand in relation to the body. Kinaesthesia provides information regarding the movement of the upper limbs, precise pressure through the handwriting instrument, and the patterns utilised to produce fast, legible script. Motor memories are established through the physical repetition of letter forms which ultimately become inherent and automatic, allowing the child to focus on comprehension and written expression.

It is possible to test the effectiveness of the kinaesthetic sense by writing your name with your eyes open, and then again with your eyes closed. If kinaesthetic feedback is intact, the signatures should look virtually identical.

Unfortunately, some children have poor proprioceptive feedback and therefore subsequent kinaesthetic memories are not established. This can cause the child to depend on other sensory modalities, in particular vision, to write effectively (Hepp-Reymond et al., 2009). This is often particularly evident in children in Key Stage 2. The reliance on vision and the focus on the pen(cil) point slows the writing process down at a time when they are required to speed up in readiness for the transition to secondary school (Copley & Ziviani, 2010). Particular handwriting difficulties seen at this stage include:

- heavy pressure through the pencil
- poor visuospatial planning
- over-reliance on vision
- reduced output speed
- focus on the process of the writing task, to the detriment of composition
- poor internal representation of the letter form
- poor sequential memory
- visual attention is focused on the pencil point.

One solution to these difficulties is to stimulate or heighten the writer's kinaesthetic and proprioceptive awareness. One way of doing this is to use static and dynamic activities and exercises that stimulate the proprioceptors of the upper limbs whilst practising movements which will reinforce letter formation and their connections in order to create words (Aman et al., 2014).

The *Speed Up!* programme (Addy, 2004) was designed for this purpose. It initially uses principles of static and dynamic resistance exercises to enhance joint and muscle position sense (Figure 53). The stimulation of muscle and joint receptors heightens the writer's awareness of their kinaesthetic sense, providing a window of opportunity in which writing patterns and then writing practice (in the form of word games) can be introduced.

Figure 53: Shoulder spirals stimulate the proprioceptors in the shoulder, elbow and wrist

The *Speed Up!* programme was not designed for children during their early years but for those aged eight and above who struggle with handwriting automaticity. Children younger than this age require the support of vision to develop early motor co-ordination. Without vision, movement time increases and movement fluency decreases in those who do not yet have a complete representation of the shape of letters (Danna & Velay, 2015). The *Speed Up!* programme was originally intended for boys with DCD who had become completely disaffected with school and handwriting in particular.

Another programme which encourages the kinaesthetic sense when forming letters is *Loops and Other Groups* by Benbow, which uses movement patterns to teach cursive writing. This programme is appropriate for children from the age of seven years old onwards. It teaches letters in groups that share common movement patterns. It includes easy-to-remember motor and memory cues to help writers visualise and verbalise the letter whilst experiencing its 'feel'. The programme recommends that students use shorter length pencils in order to help them grasp the pencil closer to the point and to facilitate a tripod grasp. This programme therefore integrates kinaesthetic, auditory and ergonomic factors.

In the next chapter we will discuss the role of motor imagery in improving handwriting skills. This involves the non-visual planning of the movement required to produce legible script. As many children with handwriting difficulties do not have accurate motor planning, the assistance of guided movements (hand-over-hand) with their eyes closed provides the kinaesthetic feedback required to plan the orientations of movement. The addition of mental imagery (where the individual is asked to close their eyes and imagine the movements required to produce a letter shape or word) can help to reinforce and embed these motor memories. The combination of guided movements which stimulate the kinaesthetic sense and motor imagery has the potential to reap positive results, with evidence that this technique can produce more significant results with older children and young people (Caeyenberghs et al., 2009; Ferguson et al., 2015; Adams et al., 2016).

Critique of the kinaesthetic approach

The principles of kinaesthetic stimulation are controversial and have been challenged by several researchers. Hepp-Reymond et al. (2009) and Aman et al. (2014) have found that it is possible to improve proprioceptive feedback through training which stimulates the muscles, whereas Sudsawad (2002) challenges the notion that handwriting can be improved through kinaesthetic training at all. Programmes such as *Speed Up!* suggest that by combining handwriting patterns with letter and word practice, and adding activities that stimulate the kinaesthetic sense, it is possible to reduce individuals' dependence on vision and enhance their writing automaticity. In the case of the *Speed Up!* programme, this requires intense practice several times each week for a period of eight weeks. However, the following results can be achieved:

Writing samples from a child aged eight years old before, halfway through and after the *Speed Up!* programme

Writing samples from a child aged 13 years old before and after the *Speed Up!* programme

(Note the reduction in pressure through the pencil.)

Summary

It is evident that legible handwriting requires the writer to have effective visual perception abilities (specifically visual-motor and visual-spatial integration), in addition to efficient kinaesthetic regulation and proprioceptive feedback. It is also unmistakable that difficulties in any of these areas can significantly impact on the automaticity of writing, but that identifying these difficulties can provide teachers with an opportunity to address any underlying issues.

Controversy abounds around the premise that the targeting of perceptual-motor and sensory-motor activities can enhance handwriting per se. What is clear is that a combination of activities which focus on developing the foundation skills of perception, dexterity, kinaesthesia and proprioception, together with overt practice of letter shapes and form, can be more motivating to young children than repetition and practice of letter forms in isolation.

The motivation quality of adopting an eclectic approach can be beneficial to all children, but particularly older children who have become disengaged with writing. Intensive interventions using less familiar techniques, which include novel kinaesthetic strategies, can be combined with motor imagery techniques to stimulate learning.

To summarise:

- *Perceptual-motor activities can change children's awareness of form, size and shape and their appreciation of spatial relationships, particularly during their early years.*
- *Perceptual-motor activities can be included in Readiness to Write programmes, providing motivating perceptual challenges while the child develops the foundation skills necessary for effective handwriting (Donica et al., 2014).*
- *Kinaesthetic stimulation can increase the awareness of the limbs to encourage writing automaticity without negating the over-reliance on vision in older children (aged eight and above), although this needs to be undertaken in parallel with direct handwriting practice.*
- *Motor imagery can be combined with kinaesthetic approaches to help those who struggle with the motor planning of orientation and movements required to produce letter shapes.*
- *Regular practice is needed for any process-orientated intervention to work. A session once a week is insufficient. Rather, two to three times per week for approximately 8–10 weeks is required to demonstrate change (Feder & Manjnemer, 2007).*

CHAPTER 5
A task-specific approach to handwriting

The task-specific (or top-down) approach focuses on the *product* of handwriting, rather than the individual components involved in the writing *process*. This approach starts by observing the individual producing a sample of handwriting and examines how this can be improved by subtle alterations and changes in practice, followed by repetition and rehearsal. It encourages a variety of experiences in order to generalise the skill (Sugden & Chambers, 1998). The use of a task-specific approach is consistent with motor learning theory and reinforces the principle that any intervention should be focused on the actual task to be learned and not the underlying components of the skill (Zwicker & Harris, 2009).

This is a more natural approach for teachers who are skilled at differentiating learning into discrete, progressive stages. However, it does require further explanation to appreciate exactly how it can be structured to support those who struggle to produce legible script.

There are four particular task-specific approaches that can be used to enhance handwriting:

1. Direct teaching
2. Cognitive-behavioural approach
3. Motor imagery
4. Ecological approach

Direct teaching

A commonly adopted task-specific approach is the direct teaching of letter formation in a systematic, structured manner, providing opportunities for rehearsal. This can be introduced in the early years and adopts a developmentally-progressive structure, providing reinforcement through positive feedback and praise.

Letters are usually taught in groups. Five letter groupings are often used:

Straight line print letters	i, l, t
Curved letters	a, c, d, e, g, o, q, s
Tunnel print letters	b, h, n, m, p, u
Diagonal line print letters	k, v, w, x, y, z
Letters that have hooks	f, j, r

The style of writing can be selected according to the school's handwriting policy; the National Curriculum does not recommend one style over another. However, it is advisable that the school has a consistent approach so that children receive guidance that is universally adopted across the school. The school may consider writing schemes such as *Nelson Handwriting* or *PenPals for Handwriting*, or font styles such as D'Nealian, Zaner-Bloser or Marion Richardson. Guidance as to which handwriting scheme is the most appropriate can be found in a regularly-updated National Handwriting Association document entitled *Choosing a Handwriting Scheme*. This provides samples from numerous handwriting programmes which can be selected and then implemented across the school curriculum.

Teachers can timetable regular lessons to support those who are struggling to write effectively; ideally, short sessions of approximately 20–30 minutes, three times each week. The use of a systematic programme enables the child or young person to practise both at school and home.

One of the questions often asked when using the direct teaching approach is whether or not to encourage the child to trace letters before copying them. There is an assumption that this is developmentally valuable. Tracing provides accurate and immediate performance feedback, whereas copying requires spatial planning and visual memorisation. The answer lies in understanding the purposes of tracing and copying. Tracing involves tracking over reference points to 'draw' the geometric forms which provide the basis of letter forms. This is fundamentally a hand–eye co-ordination exercise; the emphasis being on pencil control, rather than the production of a letter. Copying, on the other hand, demands that the child visualises the shape, memorises it and translates it below, and therefore has a visual-spatial dynamic. This is essential if the goal is ultimately for the child to produce letters without any stimulus support. Teachers therefore need to consider their rationale for using both tracing and copying.

Cognitive-behavioural approach

This approach can use teaching strategies to challenge individuals who are struggling to produce legible print to examine their own handwriting, perhaps comparing it with an ideal example. They will be encouraged to identify facets of their writing that are not clear, which they may need further guidance and support to address. The examination of the handwriting sample will not lead them to identify underlying kinaesthetic or perceptual-motor dysfunction, but will help the writer to identify and address the errors they are faced with and (in collaboration with the teacher, parent or therapist) to arrive at a solution to the highlighted need. For example, the writer may indicate that they struggle to leave an appropriate space between words when they are writing. In this case, rather than working on activities related to spatial planning, as recommended in the process-orientated approach, the writer would be encouraged to use a finger to create a space, write on grid paper or use a card spacer to help them remember how to separate words appropriately.

Intervention will usually adopt the following structure:

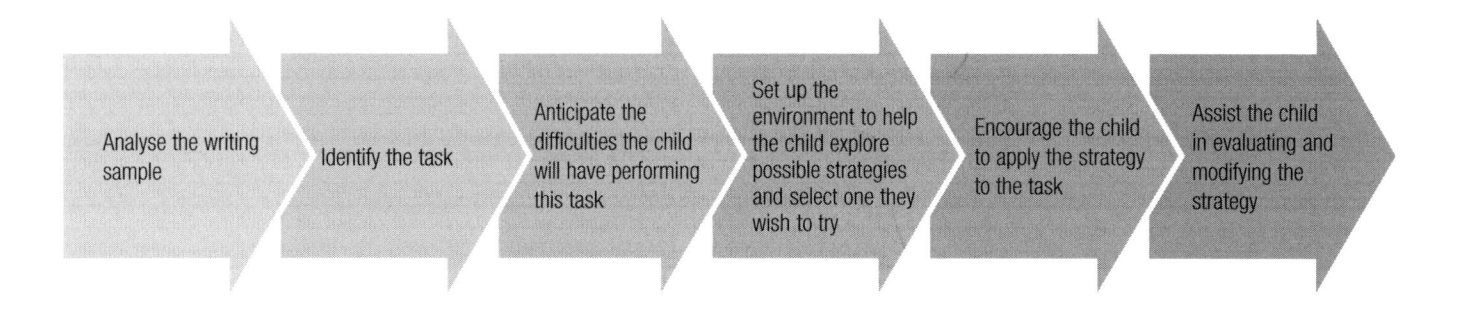

Analyse the writing sample → Identify the task → Anticipate the difficulties the child will have performing this task → Set up the environment to help the child explore possible strategies and select one they wish to try → Encourage the child to apply the strategy to the task → Assist the child in evaluating and modifying the strategy

This approach is based on Vygotsky's appreciation of the zone of proximal development, which is the difference between what a learner can do without help and what he or she can do with help. It uses a more capable peer or teacher to guide the writer into learning how to adjust their current practice to produce more legible script. The teacher will facilitate discussions as to how aspects of their writing can be adjusted and altered, and subsequently improved. This approach can be used on a one-to-one basis but also in a small group (Thornton et al., 2015).

The use of metacognition can extend this approach further. Metacognition is the awareness of one's own thought processes. This begins in pre-school and continues to improve throughout the lifespan. There are two facets of metacognition: awareness and self-regulation. This approach encourages the writer to adopt a solution-focused approach to handwriting. The writer is encouraged to analyse a sample of their own handwriting, considering what makes it legible and fluent, and which aspects could be altered or improved. This may include a comparison between their handwriting sample and an ideal script.

This approach is useful for those who are able to verbally analyse and articulate their suggestions for change, which are mediated by a capable partner or peer, parent or teacher. The writer is facilitated to identify aspects of their handwriting which may be affecting its speed and automaticity, and are then encouraged to consider strategies which may improve the process or product. The teacher plays a non-directive role and does not suggest solutions, but instead considers what the writer may need to alter to produce a fast, legible script based on their suggestions, encouraging experimentation and practice to facilitate a solution.

In order for this approach to be successful, the individual needs to be engaged and motivated to want to change their handwriting, and open to altering habits which may have been used for a prolonged period of time. They need to have good insight, a reasonable level of understanding and self-confidence to articulate their solutions to the identified issues. However, the results of this approach are extremely positive (Green et al., 2008). Nevertheless, initial engagement may be hard to acquire, especially from many boys who struggle with producing legible handwriting but who have little incentive to change.

There are five key aspects of this approach that are crucial to its success:

1 It demands cognitive analysis.
2 It entails self-instruction.
3 It involves verbal articulation and mediation.
4 It requires the adaptation of the environment, writing tools and body positioning.
5 It adopts a *goal–plan–do–review* cyclical framework.

This approach is grounded in Vygotskian principles that support the value of verbal mediation and practical experience. The strategy uses language which helps the individual to regulate and then internalise their actions and task performance (Vygotsky, 1978).

> *In all the ways we express ourselves non-verbally, none is quite as personal as our handwriting.*
> Betty Edwards

Motor imagery

Motor imagery refers to a cognitive process during which the representation of a specific motor action is mentally simulated without producing an overt body movement. In other words, the functional action is imagined. This approach is often used by sports psychologists to help professional athletes perceive how they can alter movements and actions in order to enhance their performance and speed. It has also been used with adults who have had a stroke to improve their motor skills. When using motor imagery, the individual *feels* themselves 'performing' the action rather than *doing* it (Wilson et al., 2002).

More recently, motor imagery has been used to enhance the mental representations of the multiple movement goals that handwriting demands. This approach encourages the individual to mentally simulate the required actions (i.e. the movements involved in orientating the pen(cil) around a letter shape), imagining the connections between letters to create words.

Writing, to me, is simply thinking through my fingers.
Isaac Asimov

This approach is particularly valuable for those with developmental co-ordination disorder (DCD) who struggle with aspects of motor planning, as it requires the individual to imagine moving specific body parts without the actual movement taking place (e.g. imagining the manual co-ordinates of forming the letter *e*, and its connection to forming a three-lettered word such as *end*). This imaginary planning enables the individual to predict the consequences of their actions in absence of the overt movement.

One of the difficulties in adopting this approach is that many children and young people with motor co-ordination needs affecting their handwriting may be trying to enhance skills that have not been mastered in the first place. However, there has been some positive evidence that when motor imagery is combined with kinaesthetic feedback, it can enable the writer to accurately forward plan the movements required for handwriting, reducing the errors typically seen in those who struggle with the planning and implementation of motor sequences (Blank et al., 2011).

The process involved in motor imagery has been applied to handwriting:

1 Determine the goal of the lesson (e.g. to plan how to connect the letter *c* to the letters *a* and *t* to create the cursive word *cat*) (5 mins).
2 Watch a visual extract of the selected motor skill being performed either virtually or by another person (5 mins).
3 Close eyes and mentally rehearse the motor patterns needed to replicate these connections (5 mins).
4 Overtly practise the motor skill (5 mins).
5 Alternate mental rehearsal and overt practice of the motor skill, and compare and reflect on the results (5 mins).
6 Establish a practice schedule either at home or school (5 mins).

Adapted from Adams et al. (2016)

This approach is in its earliest stages of use with children, but there has been an increase in the number of virtual reality technologies which exploit motor imagery and have been shown to facilitate motor skills in children with DCD (Hammond et al., 2014).

Ecological approach

One of the issues that many teachers face is the inconsistency in children's handwriting presentation. Teachers can be immensely frustrated when children produce virtually illegible script which contrasts with the neatness and legibility of script they produce during more formal handwriting lessons. This highlights the need to generalise skills, so that handwriting is consistently legible across a variety of settings.

The ecological approach can be adopted to encourage a consistently high level of skills in handwriting. This approach recommends that handwriting should be practised in various ways, in multiple contexts, requiring the teacher to create a high-quality writing environment with a variety of writing tools and materials available (Diamond et al., 2008). The ecological approach requires the writer to have a variety of opportunities to experiment with different types and styles of handwriting, with adult-mediated guidance to support writing development (Aram & Biron, 2004).

Research has indicated that children as young as three years old can vary their writing to represent different scenarios. For example, they can alter their writing according to whether they are depicting a treasure map, shopping list, letter or story. Young writers learn when they observe and discuss adult-modeled writing and environmental print (i.e. print that can be seen in everyday surroundings, including shop signs, advertising posters, controls on household appliances, designer labels on clothing and shop signs), and therefore quality writing instruction should be embodied in authentic writing experiences. This requires teachers to be responsive to what the child is trying to convey, supporting them in various handwriting endeavours such as labelling items, writing lists and creating child-led explanations to accompany a painting. Their writing samples will therefore reflect various contexts, changing script to reflect the task and setting. For example, a child may write their name clearly and correctly when signing a Mother's Day card, and then change their style to scribble writing during play when pretending to take an order at a restaurant, or use print to label their Lego™ construction (Purcell-Gates et al., 2007; Vukelich & Christie, 2009).

The ecological approach encourages and admits the variations in a child's handwriting, accepting that these have meaning to the individual. It encourages children to talk about not only *what* they have written but *how* they have written it. It provides various writing tools which may be used to reflect different modes of writing and encourages an environment where different handwriting styles can be practised (Bear et al., 2008). This approach extends the principles of **emergent writing**, where it is believed that every mark the child makes has meaning.

Critique of task-specific approaches

On the whole, the evidence for the use of the task-orientated, self-instruction method of addressing handwriting difficulties is positive, with changes in individuals' writing legibility evident over a relatively short period of time. However, this success is often at the expense of speed (Jongmans et al., 2003; Mackay et al., 2010).

One of the reasons for this relates back to the pen(cil) grip of those who present with handwriting difficulties. Over the time spent on the writing task, the tripod grip strength deteriorates and interferes with the handwriting process. The decrease in speed has a further bearing on handwriting automaticity, and children may be heard to say that their brain is working faster than their hand in response to comments regarding deteriorating legibility, spelling and grammar. Because of this, children have to make a choice between accuracy of formation and speed (Missenard, 2009; Weintraub et al., 2009; Engel-Yeger & Rosenbaum, 2010; Robert et al., 2010).

Although research has highlighted the benefits of adopting a task-specific, top-down approach to handwriting, it still requires a commitment to directed practice for a minimum of twice a week for ten to 20 sessions to achieve the required improvements. Intervention over a much shorter period of time appears to be insufficient (Sudsawad et al., 2002; Hoy et al., 2010).

The use of motor imagery and handwriting is still in its infancy. However, initial evaluations of combining this method of motor learning with kinaesthetic action show promising results.

When selecting any approach, it is important to take into account the child's age, cognitive ability, and their motivation to learn. These elements are crucial to the success of any intervention (Roseblum & Livneh-Zirinsky, 2008).

Summary

The top-down, task-specific approach to addressing handwriting difficulties is a natural method for teachers to adopt. This direct, graded approach forms the foundations for the teaching of most skills. It has the advantages that the teacher does not need to have a detailed understanding of the neurological processes involved in perceptual-motor development or kinaesthetic feedback, and that progress can be seen quickly.

However, the nature of task-specific approaches means that repetition and rehearsal are essential; this can cause children (particularly boys) who are disaffected with their handwriting to 'switch off'. Any intervention should therefore be presented in an enthusiastic manner with precise goals and motivational activities. Practice also needs to take place in a number of contexts (e.g. classroom, home, leisure time) so that skills are generalised.

Direct teaching is necessary and effective in the early years, with opportunities to write in environments that encourage experimentation in print, pattern and script. The detailed use of cognitive-behavioural approaches together with motor imagery is proving more successful with older children who may have established writing habits which are more resistant to change.

CHAPTER 6
When to use technology: a compensatory approach to handwriting

The value of handwriting for the development of language, reading and composition is evident. However, for some children and young people, the perceptual and motor complexities involved in producing legible script will (despite considerable intervention) be limited, and will ultimately hinder their educational progress and, more importantly, their self-esteem and confidence. For these individuals, there comes a time when an alternative to handwriting is required. This may involve the use of medium- to high-tech solutions. These should not be used as an immediate response to illegible script, but may be introduced as an adjunct to handwriting around the age of eight or nine years old, depending on the individual's need (Law et al., 2002).

The use of an alternative means of recording information requires careful consideration and must follow a detailed assessment as many of the difficulties experienced when writing will also influence skills such as keyboarding or operating apps. Care must be taken when gradually introducing alternatives, and time should be provided to evaluate whether they are indeed effective and easy to use in the classroom environment. Gierach (2009) suggests that a staged approach should be considered:

Solutions to improve aspects of handwriting

	Low-tech solutions
1	Evaluate the biomechanical aspects of writing (i.e. posture, pressure through the writing instrument, handedness, grip).
2	Evaluate the ergonomics of the environment (i.e. seating, table height, angled boards, pen(cil)s).
3	Adapt materials (raised-line paper; Ground, Grass and Sky paper; grid paper).
	Low- to medium-tech solutions
4	Use worksheets and handwriting templates (e.g. tracing and copying templates, *Fill in the blanks* activities). These can be sourced and printed to provide opportunities for practising handwriting.
5	Create a series of word banks using software. These can be used to structure sentences, reducing the need to spell out each word. They can be used on the computer or printed out.
6	Use story templates, writing guides and label makers.
	Medium- to high-tech solutions
	Try using the following:
7	A computer with word-processing software.
8	Alternative keyboards (i.e. those with large or coloured keys).
9	A portable device or word processor (e.g. tablets, notepads and iPads).
10	A computer with scanning mechanisms such as handwriting recognition software, and portable scanners.

| 11 | A computer with word prediction software. |
| 12 | A computer with voice recognition software. |

The low-tech biomechanical, ergonomic and musculoskeletal aspects of handwriting have been addressed in earlier chapters; therefore, we will now consider low- to medium-tech solutions to the production of effective handwriting, commencing at point 4 in the above table, which suggests specific resources as well as considering the usefulness of worksheets and handwriting templates. This is followed by the use of pre-written word banks to support sentence construction and the use of writing templates, before considering some of the more advanced high-tech solutions to written communication. As there are a plethora of apps and software available to support handwriting, only a few representative examples are included below which children and young people themselves have found to be helpful.

Poor handwriting costs businesses and government agencies millions of dollars annually through poorly written phone numbers, mailing addresses, tax returns, etc.
Wolf, 2011

Low- to medium-tech solutions

Worksheets and handwriting templates

There is a range of software available that can help children to observe letter formation, track letters using the interactive whiteboard, and then practise with their pencil on relevant downloaded worksheets. These include:

- *All Day to Play Literacy Suite* by Boardworks (EYFS)
- *Chinese Takeaway Role-Play Pack* by Early Vision (EYFS) – a lovely ecologically-sound writing pack
- *Left Hand Writing Skills* by Robinswood Press (EYFS–KS2)
- *Penpals for Handwriting* by Cambridge-Hitachi (EYFS–KS2)
- *Nelson Handwriting Interactive Whiteboard* CD-ROM Blue Level by Nelson Thornes (KS1–2)
- *Handwriting for Windows 3.0* by KBER (KS1–3)
- *The Handwriting Files CD-ROM* by KBER (KS1–4)
- *Precursive Fonts* by KBER (KS1–4)

Word banks

Word banks can be used to help children and young people choose words from a selection to help them construct creative sentences without the effort of physically producing each letter. This can allow writers who are so focused on the physical writing process that composition becomes secondary put this back into balance. The type of bank used will depend on the age of the child and the task being set. Key adjectives, verbs and adverbs can be provided.

On-screen word banks provide a useful technique for introducing students to word processing and writing using a computer. These can include:

- *Action Stations with Midge* by Sherston (EYFS)
- *LessonMaker Foundation v4* by Edu Tech Systems (EYFS–KS1)

- *All About Materials* by SEMERC (KS1) – for science
- *Clicker 7* by Crick Software (KS1–3)
- *IntelliTools-IntelliTalk* by Inclusive Technology (KS1–4)
- *WriteOnline* by Crick Software (KS2–4)

Story templates, writing guides and label makers

There is a wide range of software available to help children write stories using templates which use pictures, word banks and predictive text. There is also software which can help children organise their material so that it is coherent and well-structured. This is particularly beneficial for children and young people who have DCD and/or dyslexia. Label makers can be used to create worksheets which reduce the need for the individual to write extensively. They can be used to create short answer or *Fill in the blanks* worksheets. In addition, it may be possible for children and young people to use a label maker to type and print their answers to stick onto worksheets and papers, which is beneficial for short tests (e.g. on spelling or vocabulary) as it reduces the additional stress and energy expired in spelling and writing. However, bear in mind that the pupil needs to have the ability to type their answer on the label maker keyboard and manipulate the labels to get them onto their paper.

Story templates

- *Max's Toolbox* by eWord Technologies (EYFS1–KS2)
- *2 Create a Story* by 2simple (KS1–KS4)
- *Story Wizard* by I Can Write (KS2–KS4)

Writing guides

- *Kidspiration* by Inspiration Software (KS1–2)
- *Inspiration 9* by Inspiration Software (KS2–adulthood)
- *Draft:Builder* by Don Johnston (all ages)

Label makers

- *Pixel* by Inclusive Technology (KS1)
- *Clicker 7* by Crick Software (KS1–3)
- *Analysing Data* by Heinemann Explore (KS2)
- *Nutrigraph*™ by Vindogara Software (KS3–adulthood)
- *LessonKit FoodTech: Labelling* by Birchfield Interactive (KS4)
- *Designing a Package* by Birchfield Interactive (KS4)

Medium- to high-tech solutions

Computer with word processing software

It is easy to think that a transfer to word processing via a computer or laptop will provide the immediate solution to a complex handwriting problem. The reality is that the difficulties faced by children and young people who struggle to write will also influence their ability to word process. For example, the following skills are needed to be able to use a word processor:

In Great Britain, 84% of households (totalling 22 million) had computer technology in 2014, up from 57% in 2006.

- the ability to isolate fingers
- an appreciation of the layout of letters on a QWERTY keyboard
- the ability to apply adequate pressure through the fingertips
- adequate tactile perception
- effective visual-spatial planning
- accurate proprioception (the perception of pressure through the limbs)
- the ability to co-ordinate two hands together effectively
- the ability to interpret upper- and lowercase letters (typed writing may be presented in lowercase print, whereas the keys on a keyboard present uppercase letters).

The need to have accurate feedback through the fingertips is vital for effective typing. As many children with handwriting difficulties struggle with grip and the adjustment of pressure through their proprioceptive system, this will continue to be an issue when using a keyboard. Rabin & Gordon (2004) showed that the blocking of tactile feedback in the fingertips of typists led to increased typing errors, as the tactile cues which provide information about the start location of the finger are necessary to perform typing movements accurately.

In addition, visual-motor integration requires the individual to look at the screen, then the keyboard. If an individual has poor visual-motor and visual-spatial integration, they will struggle to memorise the letter required before identifying the appropriate key, hence slowing down the process of typing (Coleman et al., 2001). When considering writing on a keyboard versus handwriting, it is therefore important to assess an individual's speed and legibility in typing and writing (Preminger & Weintraub, 2004).

These are particular issues faced by children and young people who have dysgraphia and/or DCD, and therefore the transition to a keyboard will require careful planning, systematic introduction and regular opportunities for practice. It has often been found that the speed of output for both handwriting and typing is similar for these individuals. However, word processing does have the following advantages:

- The final written product tends to be neater and more legible.
- The writing process is often more efficient, since students can correct typing and spelling errors.
- The quality of their written work may be increased.
- Writing via a computer may improve individuals' attitudes towards learning to write.
- Self-esteem and confidence are raised.
- The background can be tinted to reduce visual stress; this flexibility is of particular benefit to those with a visual impairment or visual perception processing difficulty.

A further advantage of introducing children and young people to word processing is the opportunity it can provide to reflect on individual personality, which cannot be visible when handwriting is illegible. Individuals can represent their character by changing formatting options such as font styles, colour and size. Emphasis can be portrayed in bold, italic or colour.

The following programmes can help children and young people with the early stages of word processing:

Teaching typing

- *BusyFingers* by Grape County (KS1–2)
- *Mavis Beacon Teaches Typing UK Edition* by Software Mackiev (KS1–4)
- *KAZ Learn to Touch Type in Just 90 minutes V20.5* by Gotham New Media (KS1–4)
- *Typing Instructor Platinum for Kids* by Individual Software (KS2)
- *Nessy Fingers Touch Typing* by Nessy Learning (KS2–3)
- *Typing Tournament* by EdAlive (KS2–4)
- *Englishtype Joint Package* by English Type (KS2–4)

Life was much easier when apple and blackberry were just fruits!

Alternative keyboards

Dedicated time is needed to teach children and young people who have co-ordination difficulties how to use a keyboard effectively, and initially it is important to source software which introduces them to typing using both hands. Alternative keyboards which have enlarged keys, key guards and colour-coded keys can be used in the initial stages. In addition, keyboards which present lowercase letters can be helpful until the layout of the keyboard is understood.

For some children, the QWERTY keyboard is too difficult to master immediately and it may be helpful to consider an alternative before being introduced to a typical keyboard. There are several programmable keyboards that can change the appearance and function of a standard keyboard. These can include changes in the colour of the keys, font, upper- and lowercase, and the size of the keys. They include:

- *Colour Coded Kids Keyboard – Dual Case* by Hills Components (EYFS1–KS2)
- *MyKids Keyboard and Mini-Mouse Set* by Grape County (EYFS1–KS2)
- *AlphaSmart Keyguard* by Maxess Products (KS1–4)
- *Maxess Ultracompact Keyboard* by Maxess Products (KS2–4)
- *Helpikeys Keyboard* by Keytools (all ages)

Portable devices

According to Ofcom (2014), one in three children in the UK now has their own tablet computer. This number has nearly doubled since 2013; up from a fifth (19%) in 2013. Children are using tablets to communicate with friends and family (locally and across the globe), watch video clips, play games and surf the web from pre-school age onwards.

Interestingly, for the first time, the proportion of children accessing the internet on a PC or laptop fell by three percentage points year on year to 88%, in favour of accessing it on tablets and mobile phones (Ofcom, 2014). This demonstrates the increase in young people's familiarity with these portable devices and the need to highlight apps and software that can be used on these devices to support learning and written communication.

Portable notetakers are simple, lightweight computers with a keyboard interface. They allow for keyboard entry of text only and can have word prediction or text-to-speech software built in. They are usually battery-operated and therefore well-suited to the classroom, particularly in the secondary school setting.

Tablets like iPads run apps which can support students with writing tasks. These apps can assist pupils in conveying their ideas using photos, videos, voice recording and text. Pupils can have the option to use the on-screen keyboard or a physical keyboard, depending on their needs.

- *Revelation Natural Art* by Logotron (KS1–KS3)
- *Classroom Response System* by AlphaSmart (KS1–KS4)
- *10" Fusion5® Ultra Slim Tablet* by Fusion5 (all ages)
- *Forte Portable Word Processor* by Writer Learning (all ages)

Computers with scanners

Technology has advanced to such an extent that it is possible to change letters, words, sentences and paragraphs which are scanned, typed or handwritten easily and quickly to provide a clear and coherent end product. Settings can be changed to enlarge fonts, change backgrounds, and slow or speed up the response to touching the keyboard. The development of scanning software has further enhanced this process; there are now portable handheld scanners that can photograph text from books and magazines and download this directly to a computer via cable.

In addition, there are scanners that take images of handwriting and download them onto a computer, changing the handwriting into typeface. This is known as optical character recognition (OCR) technology. These devices provide massive opportunities for children and young people who struggle with handwriting, as their poorly-formed handwriting can be translated into type and later corrected if spelling or translation errors have occurred. Unfortunately however, even though technology in this area is advancing and there is now a high recognition rate for text, handwriting translation errors may remain high and the user will need to allocate time to editing script which may have 'misread' barely legible text or misspelt words. Considerable practice is needed to help the software recognise the individual's handwriting style, but with time and perseverance the conversion errors can be reduced. Unfortunately, this software struggles to decipher cursive handwriting, working better with clean print. The following are examples of scanners which can copy text and handwriting:

- *Digimemo A402* by ACECAD (KS1–adulthood)
- *OneNote* by Microsoft (KS3–adulthood)
- *FineReader* by Abbyy (KS3–adulthood)
- *QuickLink Pen Elite* by Wizcomtech LTD (KS3–adulthood)
- *MyScript® Memo* by MyScript (KS3–adulthood)
- *DigiMemo Handwriting Recognition MyScript* by ACECAD (KS3–adulthood)
- *DocuPen RC810 Portable Page Scanner* by Planon (KS3–adulthood)
- *Wizcom SuperPen – Handheld Portable Line Scanner & Translator* by Wizcomtech LTD (KS3–adulthood)
- *Digital Pen 990 02* by Staedtler (KS3–adulthood) – for digital capture of handwriting
- *Omnipage 18 Education* by Nuance (all ages)
- *Echo Smartpen* by Livescribe (all ages)

Computers with word prediction software

Word prediction software is now commonly used when sending texts from a mobile phone. This software predicts the word that the user intends to type. Over time, this prediction improves as familiar expressions and names are repeated and then recognised. Predictive text can also help children and young people who are using typing as an alternative to handwriting, especially if they are struggling to master two-handed typing. It enables those who struggle with writing to use proper spelling, grammar and word choices with fewer keystrokes, increasing quantity and efficiency and therefore reducing fatigue while maintaining motivation; freeing the creativity of individuals with motor co-ordination difficulties and dyslexia. The following are examples of excellent word prediction software typically used in the classroom:

- *Clicker 7* by Crick Software (KS1–3)
- *WriteOnline* by Crick Software (KS2–4)
- *Penfriend XL* by Penfriend (KS2–4)
- *TextThing Plus* by Topologika (KS2–adulthood)
- *Read & Write Gold Version 9* by TextHelp™ (all ages)
- *Wizkeys Plus* by Inclusive Technology (all ages)

Computers with voice recognition software

Speech recognition software is ideal for those who really struggle to produce legible script and also find typing problematic, but have lots of creative ideas they would like to record on paper. The user speaks into a microphone which is connected to the appropriate software on a computer and their words are immediately translated into text. This is intended to remove the need for motor co-ordination.

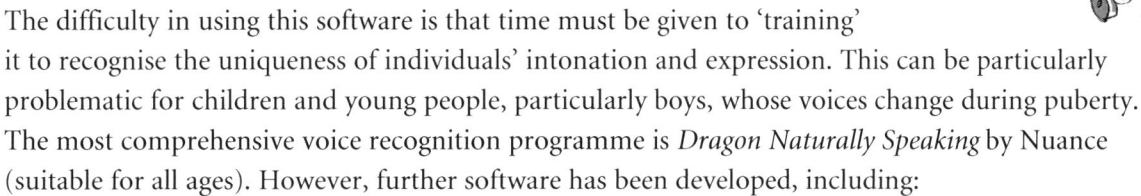

The difficulty in using this software is that time must be given to 'training' it to recognise the uniqueness of individuals' intonation and expression. This can be particularly problematic for children and young people, particularly boys, whose voices change during puberty. The most comprehensive voice recognition programme is *Dragon Naturally Speaking* by Nuance (suitable for all ages). However, further software has been developed, including:

- *KeyStone Speech Tutor* by Keyspell (KS1–adulthood)
- *ViaVoice Advanced Edition 10* by Nuance (KS3–4)
- *SpeakQ* by GoQ (all ages)
- *Windows Vista Speech Recognition* by Microsoft (all ages)
- *Olympus VN 711PC DNS* (all ages) – a portable voice recorder that links with Dragon Naturally Speaking
- *Dragon Dictate* by Nuance (all ages)

The amount of software and technical solutions available can be overwhelming; therefore, the resources suggested in this chapter are only a representative sample of those which could be used. Many companies will provide free trials and/or demonstrations, particularly when a school is considering a purchase.

Stanberry & Raskind (2009) provide excellent internet guidance regarding a range of medium- to high-tech solutions, explaining how and when they can be used. These can be accessed on the Reading Rockets and REM websites.

In addition, the UK charities AbilityNet and BDA Technology provide advice and personal assessments regarding a range of digital technology that can enable children, young people and adults to fully access the educational curriculum.

Summary

Technology has provided a solution to written recording for those whose perceptual and motor skills limit their dexterity and subsequent handwriting output. However, teachers need to be careful not to see technology as a quick solution to a complex problem. Careful evaluation is needed to ensure that each child or young person's needs are addressed on an individual basis so that the right technology is provided at the appropriate time, and ideally this should be used as an adjunct to handwriting rather than a replacement, especially during the early years.

To gain skills in either handwriting or keyboarding, an individual must have motor competence. However, the complexity of the motor co-ordination involved in either handwriting or typing differs considerably. Operating a keyboard does not provide the same kinaesthetic feedback as controlling a pencil; all that is required is pressing the right key and the movement is the same for every letter. Therefore children are not using multi-sensory pathways to remember the shapes and names of the letters they will need as they learn to read.

Previous chapters have provided evidence that during the formative years, the process of learning to write by hand is beneficial to linguistic processing, reading and composition. There is little research published as to whether word processing can reap the same rewards.

However, technology provides legible text which can be altered and corrected. This not only allows individuals to focus on composition, grammar and punctuation, but the improved presentation and legibility places their perceived competence at an equal level to their peers', improving their self-confidence, self-esteem and motivation to write.

The argument that giving up handwriting in favour of word processing and other technologies will affect how future generations learn to read will remain controversial until there is more research on the effectiveness of the use of technology in the early years. Neurologists are passionate in their desire to support the connectedness of motor, perceptual, kinaesthetic and linguistic learning on long-term cognition, especially relating to the written word. Advocates of digital technologies are convinced it makes no difference!

CHAPTER 7
Assessment and intervention

This chapter will demonstrate how to put the preceding information into practice by describing the assessments and interventions provided for a number of children and young people with significant handwriting difficulties. It will initially highlight some of the baseline assessments that can be used as outcome measures in order to evaluate the impact of the handwriting intervention. It will then present case studies, highlighting:

- the desired outcome and targets established to remediate the individual's difficulties, as recommended by the SEND Code of Practice (2015)
- the approach(es) used to address the individual's difficulties, explaining why they were adopted
- details of the resources, strategies and interventions that were used to support the budding writer.

Assessment

In order to address handwriting difficulties, it is important to first of all analyse the strengths and difficulties noted in a natural sample of the child or young person's handwriting. Observations should start by considering both the ergonomic and biomechanical factors; determining the individual's hand dominance, posture, pen(cil) grip, and positioning. The laterality table on page 24 can be used to determine handedness.

Handwriting can be analysed using either a standardised or non-standardised assessment which scrutinises a specific sample of an individual's writing. Standardised assessments are those which have been designed to measure performance against typically-developing children or young people of a given age. Samples from a large number of individuals have been evaluated for these assessments so that a 'normal' baseline can be obtained. The writer can then be measured against age-group norms or typical practice. A good standardised assessment will have involved a wide number of individuals who represent a diverse demographic population. The procedure for administering the test will be very precise and it will be possible to determine how far ahead or behind a typical population an individual is.

There are a limited number of standardised assessments of handwriting on the market in the UK, due to the variability in styles and methods used to teach handwriting in UK schools. However, the Detailed Assessment of Speed of Handwriting (DASH) is an excellent assessment for children over nine years old. The test has been evaluated on a normative sample of over 500 children nationwide. More recently, its use has been expanded by the introduction of DASH 17+, which evaluates the handwriting of young people and adults aged 17–25 years. This allows us to respond to the increased age range stipulated in the SEND Code of Practice (2015), which now extends from 0–25 years.

Detailed Assessment of Speed of Handwriting (DASH) (Barnett et al., 2007)

Age range	9–16.11 years
Content	Five subtests, including: 1 Copying the sentence *The quick brown fox...* in their best handwriting 2 Alphabet writing from memory at speed 3 Copying the sentence *The quick brown fox...* at speed 4 Graphic speed test (this involves putting crosses in circles over a period of one minute) 5 Free writing at speed (10 minutes)
Administration time	30 minutes
Available from	www.pearsonclinical.co.uk/AlliedHealth/PaediatricAssessments/PerceptualFineMotorDevelopment/DetailedAssessmentofSpeedofHandwriting(DASH)/DetailedAssessmentofSpeedofHandwriting(DASH).aspx

Detailed Assessment of Handwriting Speed 17+ (DASH 17+) (Barnett et al., 2010)

Age range	17–25 years
Content	Five subtests, including: 1 Copying the sentence *The quick brown fox...* in their best handwriting 2 Alphabet writing from memory at speed 3 Copying the sentence *The quick brown fox...* at speed 4 Graphic speed test 5 Free writing at speed (10 minutes)
Administration time	30 minutes
Available from	www.pearsonclinical.co.uk/AlliedHealth/PaediatricAssessments/PerceptualFineMotorDevelopment/DetailedAssessmentofSpeedofHandwriting/ForThisProduct/DASH17-approved-for-DSA.aspx

Other standardised measures which identify the needs of younger children have been developed in the USA. These include the following:

Evaluation Tool of Children's Handwriting (ETCH) (Amundson, 1995)

Age range	6–12.5 years
Content	Three subtests, including: 1 Seven cursive writing tasks 2 Seven print writing tasks 3 Items to assess handling of pencil and paper
Administration time	15–25 minutes
Available from	www.therapro.com/Browse-Category/Handwriting-Evaluations/Evaluation-Tool-of-Childrens-Handwriting-ETCH.html

Test of Handwriting Skills Revised (THS-R) (Milone, 2007)

Age range	5–18.11 years
Content	Eight subtests, including: 1 Writing from memory letters of the alphabet, in upper- and lowercase, and in alphabetical sequence 2 Writing from dictation letters of the alphabet, out of alphabetical order, in upper- and lowercase 3 Writing from dictation eight numbers, out of numerical order 4 Copying 12 uppercase letters out of alphabetical sequence 5 Copying ten lowercase letters out of alphabetical sequence 6 Copying six words 7 Copying two sentences 8 Writing six words from dictation
Administration time	25 minutes
Available from	www.therapro.com/Browse-Category/Handwriting-Evaluations/Evaluation-Tool-of-Childrens-Handwriting-ETCH.html

Non-standardised assessments are tests which are not based on comparisons between a similar-aged population, but which identify a specific aspect of handwriting that can be targeted with an intervention. These can include checklists, screeners, developmental profiles and criterion-referenced assessments. They can be used prior to and following an intervention to provide evidence of impact.

There are several online screeners, including the Screener for Handwriting Proficiency, which has been developed by the authors of *Handwriting Without Tears*. This is available online at: screener.hwtears.com/pdf/AdminPacket_GK.pdf

Further non-standardised assessments are provided on the following pages. These can be duplicated and used to measure the impact or change following an intervention or programme (outcome measure).

The Early Years Handwriting Assessment (Addy, 2015) can be used with children aged 4–5 years and can be completed prior to and following an intervention, with results being visually compared to each other. This assessment includes the opportunity for a child to draw themselves, which can provide an indication of the child's motor skills and the effect that this may have on their self-perception. There is evidence that children with poor motor competence have more difficulties processing proprioception, and that they consequently have a more immature body image (**schema**) than their typically-developing peers; this can be seen in their self-drawings (Proske & Gandevia, 2012; Assaiante et al., 2014). Depending on the type of intervention being provided, it is interesting to observe whether the child's self-drawing matures as the intervention progresses. Handwriting interventions which include sensory-motor activities can stimulate the proprioceptive system and enhance the child's body awareness; this in turn provides the child with improved motor awareness and subsequent control. Whether or not this affects their self-perception portrayed through their self-drawings is an interesting by-product of the intervention (Parush et al., 2009). Note that the answer to the last question on the assessment can provide you with topics that can be used to motivate the child to write.

The Handwriting Criterion-Referenced Assessment (Addy, 1995) evaluates various samples of handwriting and scores this against six criteria, providing nominal data from a potential score of 30. It is sometimes helpful for someone other than the person who is leading the intervention to complete the assessment at the beginning and again at the end to obtain an objective result. Parents or carers can be involved in this process too as it can help them to participate in the remediation process. It is advisable that the same person reassesses the individual at the end of the intervention, as the criteria can be open to personal interpretation. This assessment was used to evaluate part of the *Write from the Start* programme (Teodorescu & Addy, 1996) prior to its publication.

The Handwriting Checklist enables you to record a simple tally which identifies areas of handwriting an individual is struggling with. The tally can be compared before and after the intervention. As this checklist is quick to administer, it is a useful tool to use with a whole class.

Early Years Handwriting Assessment
(EYFS1 & EYFS2) (1)
(Addy, 2015)

Name: _____

DOB: _____

School: _____

Handedness (please tick):   Left-handed ☐   Right-handed ☐   Undecided ☐

Pencil grip (describe the grip the child usually adopts):

_____

_____

Track from left to right

Join the dots to help the girl get to the ice-cream.

Join the dots to help the boy get the ball.

Join the dots to park the car in the garage.

© Lois M. Addy 2016 | *How to identify and overcome handwriting difficulties* | LDA | Permission to photocopy

Early Years Handwriting Assessment
(EYFS1 & EYFS2) (2)

(Addy, 2015)

Can you draw the lines on the fence?

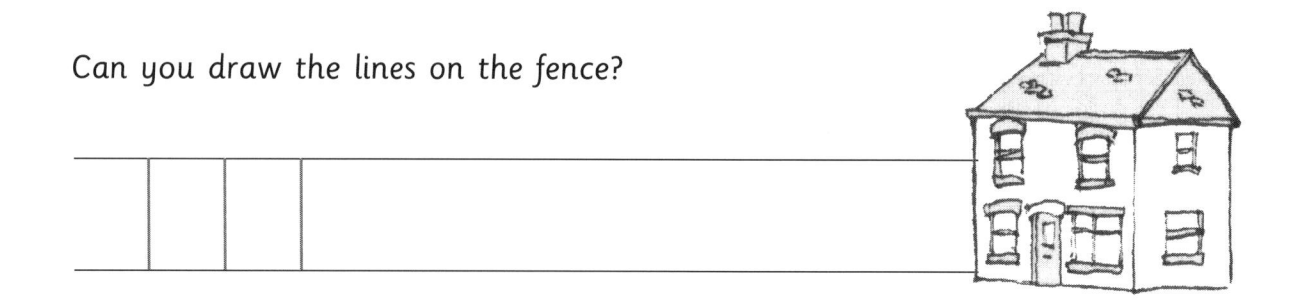

Can you join the dots to make waves?

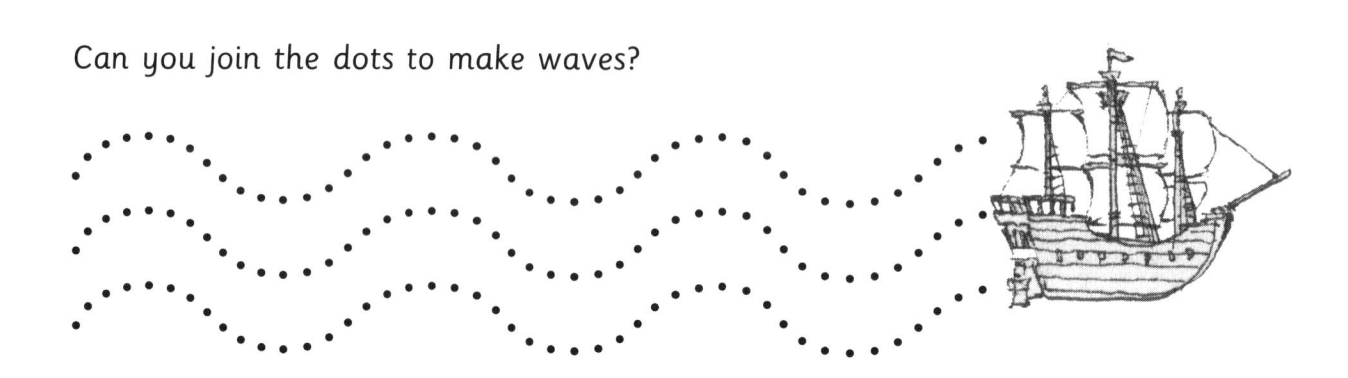

Can you put the wheels on the train carriages?

Early Years Handwriting Assessment
(EYFS1 & EYFS2) (3)

(Addy, 2015)

Copy the following shapes in the boxes below.

$\mid$	—	+	✕

L	⌐	○	C

⊃	△	□	▷

© Lois M. Addy 2016 | *How to identify and overcome handwriting difficulties* | LDA | Permission to photocopy

Early Years Handwriting Assessment
(EYFS1 & EYFS2) (4)

(Addy, 2015)

Write your name.

_____

Copy the letters of the alphabet.

a b c d e f g h i j k l m

_____

n o p q r s t u v w x y z

_____

Draw a picture of yourself in the box.

What is your favourite thing to do?

_____

_____

Handwriting Criterion-Referenced Assessment (5-13 years) (1)

(Addy, 1995)

Ask the individual to use lined paper to:

    A Write their name.

    B Copy the alphabet.

    C Write the alphabet.

    D Copy the sentence *The quick brown fox jumps over the lazy dog*.

    E Free write for five minutes on the subject 'All about me'.

Legibility

The letters and words can be clearly recognised apart from their context.

Using **A**, **B** and **C**, circle the best descriptor.

0	Attempted letters are unrecognisable as such
1	1–5 letters are recognisable when copied
2	Name is recognisable when free writing, along with 1–5 letters
3	Name is legible, and 5 additional letters are also recognisable when free written
4	Name is legible, and 10–15 additional letters are also recognisable when free written
5	All letters of the alphabet are recognisable

Accurate letter formation

The letters are formed, commencing from the line, with correct direction of flow being demonstrated.

Using **C** and **E**, circle the best descriptor.

0	All letters are incorrectly formed, despite being recognisable
1	1–5 letters are correctly formed
2	6–10 letters are correctly formed
3	11–15 letters are correctly formed
4	16–20 letters are correctly formed
5	All letters are correctly formed

© Lois M. Addy 2016 | *How to identify and overcome handwriting difficulties* | LDA | Permission to photocopy

Handwriting Criterion-Referenced Assessment (5-13 years) (2)

(Addy, 1995)

Spacing between words and letters

Spacing between words is emerging. Letters are grouped together to form appropriate words.

Using **D** and **E**, circle the best descriptor.

0	No recognisable letters and no grouping attempted
1	Few letters attempted and are recognisable but no grouping
2	Spacing reliant on copying skills
3	Attempts are made to group letters into words but spacing is erratic
4	Spaces between words are developing with only occasional errors in spatial planning
5	Appropriate spaces between words are evident

Alignment of writing on the page

Writing starts at the left-hand side of the page and transfers across the page in a left to right direction.

Using **E**, circle the best descriptor.

0	Attempted letters are unrecognisable
1	Attempted letters are placed erratically on the page
2	Letters are formatted together to create words, but do not maintain a horizontal alignment
3	Alignment across the page is attempted but writing drifts as it progresses. Further writing does not acknowledge the original starting position
4	Alignment across the page is attempted but writing drifts slightly as it progresses
5	Attempted words are constantly written from left to right in a horizontal plane

Uniformity of letter size

Letter sizes are consistent. Small letters are half the dimension of ascenders and descenders.

Using **D** and **E**, circle the best descriptor.

0	Attempted letters are illegible
1	Attempted letters are all the same size
2	Attempted letters are inconsistently small or large
3	5–10 letters are showing differentiation in size
4	4 out of the 7 ascenders (b, d, f, t, h, k, l) are sized correctly and 3 out of the 5 descenders (p, q, g, y, j) are sized correctly
5	All letters show appropriate differentiation in size

© Lois M. Addy 2016 | *How to identify and overcome handwriting difficulties* | LDA | Permission to photocopy

Handwriting Criterion-Referenced Assessment (5-13 years) (3)

(Addy, 1995)

Uniformity of letter slope

The slant of the ascending and descending letters is consistently aligned to one another, using either a backward, upward, or forward slant.

Using **D** and **E**, circle the best descriptor.

0	Attempted letters are illegible
1	Attempted letters show erratic, inappropriate directionality
2	Some ascending and descending letters show a consistent direction but this is not evident throughout the text
3	Most descending letters show a consistent direction, but the direction of ascending letters remains erratic
4	The majority of ascending and descending letters show a consistency in direction and alignment
5	All letters show consistent alignment

Total score	/30

Scores can be used to establish a quantitative base line from which handwriting objectives can be established. For example:

> Simon will increase his handwriting score from 20/30 to 27/30 over a period of two school terms.

© Lois M. Addy 2016 | *How to identify and overcome handwriting difficulties* | LDA | Permission to photocopy

Handwriting Checklist

	Observation	Yes	No
1	Does the individual seem unsure of which hand to hold the pen(cil) in?		
2	Is the pen(cil) held in an abnormal grip?		
3	Does the individual sit awkwardly on a chair when writing?		
4	Does the individual slump forward onto the table when writing?		
5	Does the individual position the paper awkwardly when writing?		
6	Does the individual lift their wrist off the paper when writing?		
7	Does the individual apply too much pressure through the pen(cil)?		
8	Does the individual apply too little pressure through the pen(cil)?		
9	Is letter formation erratic or incomplete?		
10	Is there evidence of letter reversals or inversions?		
11	Does the individual start writing away from the margin?		
12	Does the writing slope downwards or upwards across the page rather than follow a horizontal direction?		
13	Are inadequate spaces left between words?		
14	Is the sizing of letters erratic?		
15	Are letters incompletely formed (e.g. with the cross bar missing from the *t*)?		
16	Does the writing contain a mix of upper- and lowercase letters within words (e.g. *loVely*)?		
17	Do you struggle to identify distinct ascenders and descenders in the sample of writing?		
18	Does the individual struggle to join letters appropriately?		
19	Does writing appear to be laboured?		
20	Is the speed of writing slow?		
21	Does the individual have low writing confidence?		

© Lois M. Addy 2016 | *How to identify and overcome handwriting difficulties* | LDA | Permission to photocopy

Intervention

It is possible to examine an individual's handwriting by simply observing the writer and critically analysing a sample of their writing, identifying strengths and areas of difficulty. Once these have been established, an intervention plan and a specific approach can be selected.

The following case studies demonstrate the intervention process for some children and young people who have struggled to produce legible cursive writing. They show how their handwriting was analysed, their identified strengths and needs, and how objectives were established.

Intervention case study

Thomas

Age: 6.2 years

Handedness: right-handed (consistent)

Grip: lateral tripod grip

Pre-intervention handwriting sample

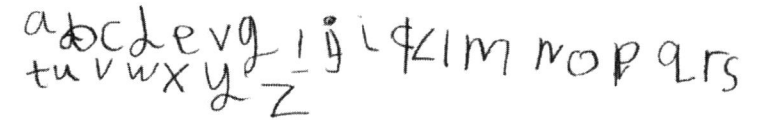

Strengths	Difficulties
Knows all letters of the alphabet except f (replaces with phonic v) and h	Incorrect formation of letters
Attempts to join letters	Mixture of upper- and lowercase letters
Relatively good alignment of writing across the page	Difficulty knowing where to join letters
	Difficulty knowing how to join letters
	No differentiation of size between upper- and lowercase letters
	Heavier pressure when attempting to join letters, demonstrating more effort

Outcome

Thomas will join letters appropriately in order to produce fluent legible script. This will be achieved within two school terms.

Targets

- To form letters correctly with the appropriate orientation and joining strokes.
- To connect letters together to create words.
- To improve the consistency of letter sizes, differentiating between upper- and lowercase letters.

Timeframe

20-minute handwriting intervention (taught) and practice (rehearsal) sessions two or three times a week in a small group for one and a half school terms, and half a term for consolidation and contextual practice.

Resources

- Reproduction of the *Write from the Start* programme (Teodorescu & Addy, 1996)
- Visual-spatial and visual-perceptual activities
- Direct handwriting practice sheets
- Angled writing board
- Dycem® matting
- Pencil grip using Loom Bands

Strategies

- Used an outline on Dycem matting to indicate correct angle of paper.
- Used Loom Bands to indicate where fingers should be placed on the pencil.

Approach

Weeks 1–14

Initially a process-orientated approach was introduced to encourage visual-spatial integration, correct orientation and size differentiation. This involved the systematic progression through *Write from the Start* in a small group, with a parent-helper trained in delivering the intervention.

The programme was supplemented with activities and games that promoted spatial planning skills (e.g. *Identify the inverted object*, *Which is the odd one out?*).

Weeks 14–21

The *Write from the Start* programme was supplemented with task-specific targeted practice in joining up writing using *Hand for Spelling Book 2* by Charles Cripps (LDA).

Weeks 21–28

An ecological approach was encouraged throughout this consolidation period. Opportunities were provided for generalising and embedding taught strategies in a variety of writing tasks.

Evaluation

Pre- and post-quantitative evaluation using the Handwriting Criterion-Referenced Scale (Addy, 1995).

Handwriting criteria	Pre-intervention score	Post-intervention score	Difference
Legibility	4	5	+1
Letter formation	4	5	+1
Spacing	3	5	+2
Alignment	4	5	+1
Letter size	2	4	+2
Letter slope	3	5	+2
TOTAL	**20**	**29**	**+9**

Post-intervention handwriting sample

Intervention case study

Ahmed

Age: 6.8 years

Handedness: right-handed (inconsistent)

Grip: lateral tripod grip

Pre-intervention handwriting sample

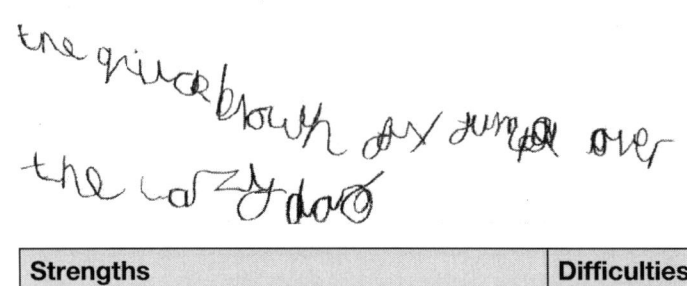

Strengths	Difficulties
• Knows all letters of the alphabet except *h* • Attempts to join letters • Relatively good letter formation • Reasonable pressure through the pencil point	• Mixture of upper- and lowercase letters • Reversals and inversions are evident with the letters *f/t, j/l, b/d* • Attempts to join all letters, without appreciating pencil lifts • Erratic alignment of writing across the page • No differentiation of size between upper- and lowercase letters • Evidence of motor overflow (where there is little appreciation of where a letter starts or stops)

Outcome

> Ahmed will join letters appropriately, appreciating when to lift the pen(cil) in order to produce fluent legible script. This will be achieved within two school terms.

Targets

- To appreciate correct letter orientation and joining strokes.
- To appreciate when to insert pen(cil) lifts when joining letters to produce words.
- To improve the consistency of letter sizes, differentiating between upper- and lowercase letters.
- To encourage a clear start and end point of each letter and word (reducing overflow).

Timeframe

10-minute handwriting intervention and practice sessions two or three times a week in a small group for one and a half school terms, and half a term for consolidation and contextual practice.

Resources

- Orientation activities (e.g. *Which is the wrong way round?*, *Which is the inverted object?*, SEMERC's Letter Olympics)
- Reproduction of the *Write from the Start* programme (Teodorescu & Addy, 1996)
- Reproduction of cursive worksheets from Kidzone at www.kidzone.ws/cursive/index.htm
- PenAgain ergonomic pencil
- Pattern blocks and board set
- Perceptual worksheets such as *Which object is inverted?*

Strategies

- Interspersed handwriting sessions with small-group orientation games.
- Prompted Ahmed to use right hand for writing.

Approach

Weeks 1–21

A combined process-orientated and task-specific approach was used. *Write from the Start* was introduced. This was interspersed with the direct teaching of cursive handwriting.

Lessons were provided in a small group and delivered by a combination of class teacher, class TA and a parent-helper trained in administering the intervention.

The programme was supplemented with activities and games which promoted spatial planning skills (e.g. *Identify the inverted object*, *Which is the odd one out?*, SEMERC's Letter Olympics).

Weeks 22–28

Consolidation was provided by ensuring that there were multiple opportunities for writing practice. Reminders were given to reinforce previous teaching.

Evaluation

Pre- and post-quantitative evaluation using the Handwriting Criterion-Referenced Scale (Addy, 1995).

Handwriting criteria	Pre-intervention score	Post-intervention score	Difference
Legibility	3	5	+2
Letter formation	4	4	0
Spacing	2	5	+3
Alignment	3	5	+2
Letter size	3	4	+1
Letter slope	3	5	+2
TOTAL	**18**	**28**	**+10**

Post-intervention handwriting sample

Intervention case study

Matthew

Age: 11.2 years

Handedness: left-handed (consistent)

Grip: dynamic tripod grip and lateral tripod grip (alternates between two grips during task)

Words per minute (WPM): 12

Pre-intervention handwriting sample

Strengths	Difficulties
Most letters are legible	Heavy pressure through the pen
Attempts to join letters	Erratic alignment of ascending and descending letters
Spatial planning is reasonable	Difficulty knowing when to lift pen (tends to join all letters)
	Legibility deteriorates when Matthew attempts to write faster
	Tendency to smudge writing
	Writing lacks fluency

Outcome

> Matthew will join letters effectively, appreciating when to lift the pen, in order to produce fluent, legible and fast script. This will be achieved within ten weeks.

Targets

- To appreciate when to insert pen lifts when joining letters to produce words.
- To reduce pressure through the pen and increase writing fluency.
- To improve the alignment of ascending and descending letters.
- To encourage a clear start and end point of each letter and word (reducing overflow).
- To improve speed of output.

Timeframe

Attendance at handwriting intervention group once a week for ten weeks, with further individual practice three times a week for ten minutes each time.

Resources

- Angled writing board
- Dycem matting
- *Speed Up!* writing programme (Addy, 2004)
- *Speed Up!* writing board and chalk
- Materials recommended in *Speed Up!* programme (i.e. sugar paper, crayons, paints, fibretip pens, light-up pens)
- TheraBand™ strap

Strategies

- Used Dycem matting to indicate optimum position of hand and paper when writing.
- Used a light-up pen to regulate pressure when writing at speed.
- Placed TheraBand strap around base of chair to keep feet on the floor and secure postural stability.

Approach

Weeks 1–10

The *Speed Up!* kinaesthetic writing programme was introduced in a small group. The latter part of this programme introduces task-specific games to develop handwriting speed.

Lessons were delivered by a combination of specialist teacher, class advanced teaching assistant (ATA) and parent-helper trained in running the intervention.

Evaluation

Evaluation consisted of pre- and post-intervention natural handwriting samples (taken from an exercise book) and words per minute.

Post-intervention WPM: 23 (+11)

Post-intervention handwriting sample

6th September, 2006

Homework

Select an individual who you think has played an important part in history. Explain briefly what they did and why you think they are important.

Nelson

Horatio Nelson was born in Norfolk in the parish of Burnham Thorpe. Young Nelson entered the navy as a midshipman at the age of 12. When war broke out with revolutionary France in 1793 he became comander of a 68 gun ship called Agamemnon then in the Mediterranean. He lost his sight in his right eye in 1794 in the siege of Calvi on the island of Corsica. In 1797 he lost his right arm when attacking santa cruz de Tenerfe in the Canary Islands.

Nelson fought in wars in Egypt and Copenhagen. lateer he was sent to fight with a fleet in the Mediterranean. He blockaded the French fleet at Toulon for a year until they got out Nelson chased them to West Indies and back, then attacked them and there allys in the harbor of Cádiz and destroyed them at the cape of Trafalgar on Oct 21, 1805. From his ship he flew the signal that has been Britain's Watchword: "England expects that every man will do his duty."

Intervention case study

Miranda

Age: 9.2 years

Handedness: right-handed (consistent)

Grip: lateral tripod grip

WPM: 15 (but legibility impaired)

Pre-intervention handwriting sample

Strengths	Difficulties
• Miranda has lots of ideas for her writing • Can differentiate between upper- and lowercase letters • Is starting to join letters in a cursive style	• Poor alignment of the writing on the page (unsure of where to start each line) • Mixture of print and cursive writing • Difficulty reading writing out of context • Incomplete letter formation • Erratic spatial planning (unclear spaces between words when printing)

Outcome

> Miranda will produce fast, legible script, obtaining a minimum of 20 legible words per minute. This will be achieved within 16 weeks.

Targets

- To obtain a balance between speed and legibility.
- To commence writing at the margin, improving writing alignment.
- To form and orientate letters appropriately.
- To write using a consistent cursive script.

Timeframe

Attendance at handwriting intervention group after school once a week for ten weeks, with further individual practice two times a week for ten minutes each time. Followed by one-to-one guidance once a week for six weeks.

Resources

- *Speed Up!* writing programme (Addy, 2004)
- *Speed Up!* writing board and chalk
- Materials recommended in *Speed Up!* programme (i.e. sugar paper, crayons, paints, fibretip pens, light-up pens)
- Timer or stopwatch

Strategies

- Used a light-up pen to regulate pressure when writing at speed.
- Practised repeated writing of a nursery rhyme in three-minute blocks two times a week to increase speed and legibility against the clock.

Approach

Week 1

Assessment of handwriting in three different scenarios: best attempt, writing at usual pace, and writing at speed.

Weeks 2–9

The *Speed Up!* kinaesthetic writing programme was introduced in a small group. The latter part of this programme introduces task-specific games to develop handwriting at speed, but with clear legibility.

Week 10

Re-assessment and discussion around next steps. During this week, Miranda's handwriting was reviewed and compared with her baseline sample. Together, we discussed the next steps and decided that a targeted approach would help to address some of the particular difficulties she was facing when joining certain letters.

Weeks 11–16

Task-specific approach adopting the cognitive-behavioural method to address identifiable concerns, which were subsequently targeted through direct action and rehearsal.

Lessons were delivered by a combination of specialist teacher and class ATA.

Evaluation

Evaluation consisted of pre- and post-intervention natural handwriting samples (taken from an exercise book) and words per minute.

Post-intervention WPM: 26 (+11)

Post-intervention handwriting sample

Finding the time to address handwriting difficulties

Finding the time to address the specific concerns of those who have handwriting difficulties can be particularly challenging due to the complex demands of the National Curriculum. However, the importance of establishing these skills in the early years cannot be underestimated, and therefore providing dedicated time to teach them is essential.

Many schools have eliminated all priority and time for specific instruction of handwriting, and college methods courses for teacher training rarely touch on handwriting due to a belief that it will shortly become an obsolete skill (Young et al., 2015). We therefore need to promote the collection of evidence which strongly indicates that the instruction of handwriting not only enables written expression but also enhances manual dexterity, perceptual development, and cognitive and linguistic skills, particularly during the early years.

Since handwriting is a complex skill, teachers must allocate time to employ effective instructional techniques for pupils to learn the precise movements required to write letter shapes while introducing them to the letter sounds and connections within a word, building in time for experimentation and practice (Blazer, 2010). Careful classroom management is needed to allocate approximately three 20-minute sessions per week to handwriting; most interventions require approximately 16 sessions to show meaningful results.

The question of who can deliver a specific intervention is important. Teachers will often be concerned that they personally cannot allocate the time needed to address a child's individual difficulties, even though they know that this is needed. Dockrell's research (2015) found that teachers confessed to enjoy teaching writing and felt prepared to teach it. However, despite feeling that they were effective in identifying approaches to support students' writing, nearly half reported that supporting struggling writers was problematic for them. This was occasionally due to their own feelings of inadequacy in knowing how to address the problem. Indeed, very few teachers are taught how to teach handwriting during their initial teacher education. This results in them introducing handwriting on the basis of how they themselves were taught, which can cause children to experience an eclectic mix of styles from one class to another. While creativity in developing a personal writing style is to be encouraged, there is also a need for a consistent approach and style to be introduced, especially in a child's early years (Arslan & Ilgin, 2010).

Specific handwriting interventions can be undertaken by anyone who clearly understands the rationale for the suggested approach and its mode of delivery. This may be a teacher, older pupil, teaching assistant (TA) or parent-helper. The empowerment and use of the people who surround a child adopts an approach known as **asset-based delivery**.

The asset-based delivery model was initially established in the US to address problems experienced by communities with social and economic need. Previous attempts to address social issues adopted a needs-based problem-solving approach which engaged professional expertise and external resources with limited long-term benefits (Mathie & Cunningham, 2003). The asset-based delivery approach altered the focus by analysing and then engaging the capacities, talents, skills, buildings, facilities, organisations and financial resources located within the community to resolve the community's own need (Kretzmann & McKnight, 1996).

The asset-based delivery approach works on the premise of optimism, identifying the skills and expertise that are internally available, rather than focusing on support from external experts (or the availability of a specialist teacher or SENCo in a school setting). The starting position is one of

'*Who do we have and what assets are already available to us to address this need?*'. These may include personnel, space and resources. Once these qualities have been identified, these are reviewed and discussions can take place as to who can take on which role, which resources are available and which resources are still required, and so on. This is known as **asset mapping** (Pan et al., 2005).

The asset-based approach has been used to address the handwriting needs of several groups of children in North Yorkshire who attended small rural schools where staffing was limited. In one example, the school was encouraged to harness a team of parent-helpers, who could offer one or two hours support a week. Following training in the desired handwriting intervention, they were asked to organise the intervention to be delivered a minimum of three times a week for ten weeks. Each session was approximately 20–30 minutes long.

These parent-helpers had a variety of backgrounds and expertise, but by empowering and enabling them to organise this, they created a rota of helpers who could deliver the intervention to groups of six children with complex handwriting needs. Natural leaders emerged, and some helpers were on standby to step in in the event of sickness or an altered programme, whilst other helpers created rewards charts and stickers to motivate the children throughout the intervention.

Results for the children were positive, as seen in the table below. They were measured using the Handwriting Criterion-Referenced Scale (Addy, 1995).

Child	Pre-intervention TOTAL	Post-intervention TOTAL	Difference
A	20	29	+9
B	20	23	+3
C	20	21	+1
D	18	17	-1
E	11	23	+12
F	18	28	+10

Results for the asset-based delivery team were very empowering and comments demonstrated their understanding of the process:

I loved the fact that I was entrusted to deliver this programme. Normally, I sit and read with the children; this has given me the opportunity to learn new skills and support my own children with aspects of handwriting.

I made sure that he always had freedom on his left-hand side and wasn't scrunched up next to someone. I would make sure that the position of paper was on an angle at a position he was comfortable with. I am left-handed too, so I was more aware of the issues he could face regarding posture and positioning.

No-one usually asks what we do as parents. I was thrilled to be able to use my graphic design skills to create certificates for the children undertaking this programme.

I tried to make sure the environment and seating were appropriate when I started.

Giving positive encouragement was so important. The children were particularly pleased when they could look back to the beginning of their books and see their progress.

Other asset-based delivery programmes have engaged local initial teacher education (ITE) students, sixth form students and peers in delivering the interventions, following training. This approach has been advocated more recently by Zurcher (2016), who states that 'if writing skills really are this essential, teachers and administrators must seek creative solutions to find time to develop students into effective writers'. This must include the initial ability to produce legible script.

> Parents are a 'powerful, underused source of knowledge'.
> Nistler & Maiers, 2000

Summary

This chapter has demonstrated the uniqueness of children's handwriting difficulties and the need to personalise interventions in response to their motor and perceptual abilities whilst taking into account their motivation to learn.

The SEND Code of Practice (2015) constantly refers to the importance of establishing clear outcomes with SMART goals. This should apply to all learning needs, including handwriting. This chapter has therefore shown how it is possible to identify a pupil's strengths and needs and then obtain an objective measure of their typical writing performance. This can provide both qualitative and quantitative data from which to measure progress.

There is a plethora of handwriting programmes available to teachers and it is only through the establishment of transparent outcomes with identifiable targets and clear timelines that the effectiveness of these programmes can be realised. As more teachers adopt this practice, it will become possible to be more critical about what does and doesn't work with certain children and young people.

The challenge of including regular handwriting practice in the school day requires careful classroom management. Teachers are under pressure to teach a wide and detailed curriculum with limited time and resources. Creative solutions to practising handwriting are needed. The asset-based approach has proved beneficial to many children.

What is clear is that while many children can master the complexities of handwriting with relative ease, 10–30% of children do not (Feder & Manjnemer, 2007). If between three and nine children in a typical UK class of 30 struggled with an aspect of the curriculum such as maths or reading, dedicated time would be allocated to ensure they were supported. It is no less important that dedication is given to those pupils who are struggling to master handwriting, an essential recording skill, so that they are free to unleash their imagination and ideas alongside their peers.

> *Poets don't draw. They unravel their handwriting and then tie it up again, but differently.*
> Jean Cocteau

CHAPTER 8
Conclusion

The importance of handwriting as a motor, perceptual and cognitive skill is evident when its component skills are analysed. Neurologists and cognitive psychologists are active in promoting the continued value of handwriting as an essential skill for the development of language and literacy, showing that during the early years, children who write by hand produce more words and generate more ideas than those who use keyboards or other digital technology (Bosga-Stork et al., 2015; Wollscheid et al., 2016).

Opponents argue that handwriting is no longer relevant and classroom instruction is better devoted to other subjects, including digital proficiency. Advocates of typing have also maintained that typing allows students to focus upon the planning of writing, proper use of grammar, and the composition of writing, rather than the mechanics of handwriting (such as how to form letters correctly).

The reality is that both handwriting and technology have their place in the classroom. In early childhood, handwriting is a necessary skill for providing the foundations from which language and literacy will emerge. This will provide the skills required to produce higher-order composition, for which technology can be used to enhance spelling, grammar and punctuation.

For pupils who struggle to master the components of handwriting, targeted support can effectively address the aspects of motor co-ordination, perception and language they struggle with and latterly, technology can be used to compensate for specific limitations. This is especially appropriate for those with dysgraphia and developmental co-ordination disorder (DCD) who, despite having the potential to make considerable progress with regards to writing presentation and legibility, may never be able to produce the same volume or legibility of writing at speed as their peers.

To stimulate changes in schools, there is a need for co-operation between teachers and researchers. If there is a chance to demonstrate conclusively that handwriting and reading skills are linked by fluency, researchers need data from teachers. If there is to be hope that people with written language disabilities can be helped, teachers need input from researchers (Young et al., 2015).

> *Handwriting competency is not only important for academic success at school age, but it is a critical skill throughout adulthood... It is especially important that health practitioners and educators appreciate the far-reaching academic and psychosocial consequences of poor writing. This immediate form of communication continues to be an essential skill both inside and outside the classroom, despite the widespread use of technological devices.*
>
> Feder & Majnemer, 2007

A final word

My penmanship is pretty bad.
My printing's plainly awful.
In truth, my writing looks so sad
It ought to be unlawful.

I try but, still, I must confess
my writing looks like scribbles.
My pencil makes a painful mess.
My ballpoint leaks and dribbles.

My letters take up so much space
they nearly can't be read.
The ones that should be lowercase
are capitals instead.

My p's and q's and R's and b's
are backward half the time.
When letters look as bad as these
it's probably a crime.

My cursive's utter lack of style
will make you want to curse.
But, even so, I have to smile;
my teacher's writing's worse.

By Kenn Nesbitt

APPENDIX A
Pelvic girdle stability activities

These are activities which work the muscles around the hips to help the individual stabilise their trunk in order to control their upper limbs to write effectively. These activities can be included in class PE lessons.

Floor football

Two teams of approximately eight players are positioned on a 'pitch' (i.e. in the sports hall). Some are positioned in defence to protect the goal, others are in attack and are positioned on their opponents' side, facing the goal. The teams sit on the floor and are not allowed to move from their chosen position. They use their arms to push the ball (which must be kept under shoulder height) to score a goal. The ball should not be passed or caught; rather, the arms should be used to flip or push the ball towards the goal.

Seated volleyball

Two teams of approximately eight to ten players sit on the floor either side of a volleyball net. The net is lowered and the game is played from this position using either a balloon or beach ball instead of a volleyball.

Crab football

Two teams of approximately eight players position themselves facing the direction of their respective goal (some in a forward attack position, and some in a defensive position). Children assume a 'crab' position (Figure 54) and attempt to dribble and kick a football into their opponents' goal. This game is exhausting so it should only be played in short five-minute bursts.

Figure 54: The crab position

Railtrack waddle

Draw two tracks in chalk on the ground, approximately 15cm apart. Children stand and have to rock backwards and forwards with their feet outside the track to the end of the rail. Add to this game as follows:

© Lois M. Addy 2016 | *How to identify and overcome handwriting difficulties* | LDA | Permission to photocopy

- In pairs, hold onto the leader by the hips and waddle along the track by rocking to either side in a synchronised manner.
- Add a 'carriage' (as above, but with extra members adding to the train).
- In pairs with one of the pair facing forwards and the other facing backwards.
- Widen the track and repeat the games described above.

Jousting

Children get in pairs. Each player holds a 'joust' (a roll of newspaper) in one hand and a paper plate held in a tray position in the other. Each player must assume a hopping position and try to knock the tray out of their opponent's hand using the joust.

Walking on stilts

Create stilts using strong tin cans (such as paint cans) and strong twine or rope. Attempt to meander around an obstacle course, emphasising skill rather than speed (this is less dangerous!).

Wii Balance Board™

The Wii Fit™ has a particularly good range of activities which can promote balance, and in doing so improve hip stability. There is evidence of its effectiveness in promoting co-ordination (Momberg et al., 2013; Jelsma et al., 2014).

Rock and throw

Children get in pairs and practise throwing and catching a beanbag to one another while balanced on a balance board. Vary the challenge to include throwing and catching a balloon, soft ball, beach ball, football or basketball; throwing through a hoop; throwing to hit a target; and (latterly) attempting head or catch. This is where a central player passes the ball calling out 'head' or 'catch', and the player they are passing it to must respond accordingly. The opposite can make the game harder (and more fun): when 'head' is called, the recipient must catch the ball, and when 'catch' is called, the recipient must head the ball back to the central player.

Maze balance board

Rather than purchasing a plain balance board, a maze version (Figure 55) can be purchased to encourage accurate balance and hip stability. The user must try to move the board carefully using precise hip movements to manoeuvre a ball around the balance board maze.

Hopscotch

Use chalk to draw a hopscotch pattern on the ground. Each player has a marker such as a stone. The first player stands behind the starting line to toss their marker in square one. They start by hopping over square one to square two and then continue hopping to square eight, turn around, and hop back again. Then continue by tossing the stone in square two, and so on.

Figure 55: A maze balance board

Kneeling throw and catch games

Provide each player with a soft cushion or rubber mat to kneel on. Introduce various throwing and catching games from a kneeling position.

Superman/Superwoman

Get children to lift their upper body, arms and legs off the ground whilst lying on their stomach. This should look as though the child is flying or free-fall parachuting. Aim for children in EYFS1–Year 2 to hold the position for ten seconds and children in Year 2 onwards to hold for 20–60 seconds.

Point kneeling challenges

Get children to start off in a 4-point crawling position and:

- lift their right arm out and hold this position for a count of ten
- lift their left arm out and hold this position for a count of ten
- lift their right leg out and hold this position for a count of ten
- lift their left leg out and hold this position for a count of ten
- lift their left arm and right leg out and hold this position for a count of ten
- lift their right arm and left leg out and hold this position for a count of ten.

Or for more challenging exercises they could:

- lift their right arm and right leg out and hold this position for a count of ten
- lift their left arm and left leg out and hold this position for a count of ten.

French cricket

One child (the 'batter') stands in the centre of a large gym hall or small field with a cricket bat which will be used to protect their lower legs. The rest of the class take it in turns to try to throw a soft ball or tennis ball to touch the area between the batter's knees and ankles. If the ball touches this area, the batter is out and a new one is selected.

Wall slide

Ask children to stand with their backs against a wall and, without using their hands, slowly slide down to a crouching position and then stand up again. They should attempt this ten times.

Partner squat

As above, but standing back-to-back with a partner with their arms entwined. They should attempt to slowly squat down, hold this position for five seconds, and then stand up again. They should attempt ten squats.

Kung-Fu stork

Get children to balance on one leg with their other leg bent in front of them. Challenge them to hold a ball out in front with straight arms, attempt to squat down slightly on one leg and then stand up again without losing balance. They should attempt five squats.

Bridging

Ask children to lie on their backs, with their knees bent and feet flat on the floor (Figure 56). Tell them to push hard through their heels to raise their bottom off the floor to create a bridge. Aim for children in EYFS1–2 to hold the position for five seconds and children in Year 2 onwards to hold for ten seconds. Repeat five times.

Figure 56: The bridge position

Chin-chin

Ask children to lie on their backs with their knees bent and feet flat on the floor. Place a beanbag between their knees and get them to lift up both knees together to drop the bean bag under their chin.

Pass the bean bag

Ask children to lie on their backs in a row with knees bent. The first child in the row must try to pick up a beanbag with their feet and pass it to the next person, who then passes it to the next person. This can be undertaken as a race with several teams involved. No hands should be used.

Older pupils can attempt these activities using a TheraBand™ strap, as stipulated in the TheraBand manual (available online at www.thera-band.com/userfiles/file/resistance_band-tubing_instruction_manual.pdf).

APPENDIX B
Shoulder girdle stability activities

These are activities which add strength to the shoulder girdle, providing stability when writing. Activities have been divided into those that can be undertaken in the classroom before any writing task begins and those that can be included in a class PE lesson.

In the classroom

Arm spirals

Ask children to hold their arms out horizontally to the sides of their body and start by making small circles, very slowly, that become bigger and bigger. Then ask them to change direction and reduce the size. Attempt five in each direction.

Wall press-ups

Get children to stand approximately one metre away from a wall and place their arms against the wall at a height parallel to the shoulders, then lean forward to touch their nose on the wall (Figure 57). They should attempt ten wall press-ups.

Figure 57: Wall press-ups

Graffiti wall

Place a long strip of paper along a wall at children's eye height. Select an appropriate theme (e.g. spring) and ask children to write or draw images to reflect this theme. This will involve considerable shoulder strength, but is highly motivating.

Cave drawing

Place a sheet of paper under the table. Ask children to lie on their backs underneath the table and complete a prehistoric drawing or painting on the paper while maintaining this position.

Mirror, mirror

Ask children to get into pairs and sit facing each other. One child makes upper limb movements and their partner copies them. After a short while they swap leadership.

Clean the floor

Ask children to stand with their feet a little apart and lean over with their legs straight. They should start to create small circles with their hand on the floor as though they are polishing it, allowing the circles to get bigger and then smaller. Get them to swap hands and repeat the process again.

In class PE lessons

Rescue

You will need some old large bath towels or small blankets for this activity. Ask children to get in pairs. One will lie on the blanket and the other must 'rescue' them by pulling them on the blanket from one end of the room to the other. Note that this will only work on a polished PE floor, not carpet. If it is too much effort for one child to pull another alone, two children can come to the rescue.

Wheelbarrow races

Children get into pairs and assume a wheelbarrow position, then race across the room in this position. Alter this task by inserting obstacles to meander around.

Scooter board relays

One child lies on a scooter board and scoots to the end of the room using their arms. Games can include the following:

- Carry a bean bag on the scooter, scoot to the end and throw the beanbag into a bucket.
- Scooter race with obstacles.
- Scooter tag can be played with four players all lying on a scooter board each, attempting to rescue a flag and return with it to their corner of the room.

Parachute activities

All of the games played with parachutes are effective in strengthening the upper limbs. These can include the following:

Making waves

Children can make small, medium or large movements to make various types of 'waves'. Incorporate sea shanty songs such as *The big ship sailed on the ally, ally oh*; *A sailor went to sea, sea, sea*; *Bobby Shaftoe's gone to sea*; *My Bonnie lies over the ocean*; *If all the seas were one sea*; *When the boat comes in*.

Bubblegum bounce

Place a number of small lightweight balls onto the parachute. Shake it to make them jump up (like the movement of bubblegum balls when coming out of a bubblegum machine).

Ball roll

Place a number of small lightweight balls onto the parachute. Try to roll the balls into the hole in the middle of the parachute. Alternatively, try to stop the balls falling through the hole in the centre.

Parachute tag

Lift the parachute high into the air. Call out two children's names. They must swap places before the parachute comes down and 'catches' them. They can run, skip, hop, twirl or crawl for variation.

Who in the group…?

Call out 'Who in the group…?' and complete the sentence with a fact (e.g. 'Who in the group had cornflakes for breakfast?', 'Who in the group has a birthday in March?'). Children who can answer the question in the positive must swap places under the parachute before it comes down on top of them.

Tent

Give each child in the group a number, then lift the parachute high, count to three and call out either *odd* or *even*. Children with this kind of number must get under the tent and sit down before the parachute comes down on top on them.

Rollerball

Try to keep a ball rolling along only the outer edge of the parachute around the circle. As it comes towards them, they must co-operatively lower their edge, then raise it when it is just past them. Then they must try changing the direction of the ball.

Find the shoe

Give every child a number then ask each child to remove one shoe and put it in a pile under the parachute in a central position. When the parachute is raised, call out two numbers. The children with those numbers must dash under the parachute, find their shoe and head back to their place before the parachute lands on top of them.

Hands and feet obstacle course

Place children in teams of between four and six. Each team member draws around their hands and feet. Each team then creates a pathway by placing these drawings of hands and feet onto the floor with tape or Blu-Tack in a random fashion across the room. The other teams must try to cross the room by placing their hands and feet on the outlines as they move across. Note that the team creating the course must also be able to transition across the room using their course.

Elbow plank

Get children to lie on the floor face down with their elbows bent and tucked into the side of their body. Ask them to lift their body up to make an angled plank and hold it for as long as possible, before resting.

APPENDIX C
In-hand manipulation activities

These activities can be used to warm up the hand in readiness for writing.

Finger songs

Including *Tommy thumb*; *Two little dickie birds sitting on a wall*; *Five little ducks went swimming one day*; and *1, 2, 3, 4, 5, once I saw a fish alive*.

Collage crumple

Crumple small pieces of tissue paper using one hand to make a simple collage.

One-handed origami

Attempt to make a simple origami boat or flag using only one hand.

Bug catcher

Place some dry pasta tubes or bows in a sand tray and try to pick them out using large tweezers. This game could be timed and the pasta pieces could vary in size.

Hidden treasure

Hide small pegs in a sand tray and ask children to find ten pegs using only one hand. All of the pegs should be held in one hand at the same time.

Sorting the buttons

Provide a child with a tray of mixed buttons and a series of jars. The child must sort the buttons as quickly as possible according to colour or size.

Squirrelling

Using the fingertips, turn a coin from heads to tails ten times with only one hand, as fast as possible (Figure 58). Manoeuvre the coin from the palm to the fingertips and back again ten times. Try to thread the coin between the fingers from index to little finger, and back again.

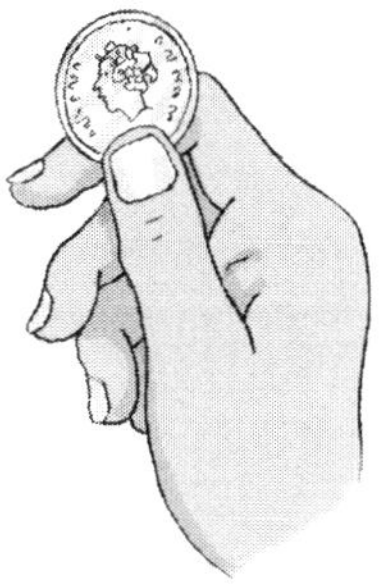

Figure 58: 'Squirrelling'

Shift

Ask a child to hold a pencil at its base and move their hand up to the point by shifting it up using their fingers, then shift down again. Repeat ten times.

Rotate

Rotate a pencil 360º in a windmill motion using one hand. Attempt this ten times.

Translation

Roll a pencil placed horizontally in the palm to the fingertips and back again. Attempt this ten times.

REFERENCES

Adams ILJ, Steenbergen B, Lust JM & Smits-Engelsman BCM (2016). Motor imagery training for children with developmental co-ordination disorder – study protocol for a randomised controlled trial. In *BMC Neurology*, 16 (5). doi: 10.1186/s12883-016-0530-6.

Addy LM (1995). The Evaluation of the Teodorescu Perceptuo-Motor Handwriting Programme. MA Thesis. York University.

Addy LM (2004). Speed-Up Handwriting Programme. Hyde. LDA.

Alonzo MAP (2015). Metacognition and sensorimotor components underlying the process of handwriting and keyboarding and their impact on learning: an analysis from the perspective of embodied psychology. In *Social and Behavioral Sciences*, 176: 263–269.

Aman JE, Elangovan N, Yeh IL & Konczak J (2014). The effectiveness of proprioceptive training for improving motor function: a systematic review. In *Frontiers in Human Neuroscience* 8: 1075. doi: 10.3389/fnhum.2014.01075.

Amundson S (1995). Evaluation Tool of Children's Handwriting (ETCH). Homer. OT Kids Inc.

Amundson S (1998). TRICS for Written Communication. Pocket Full of Therapy. Homer. OT Kids Inc.

Amundson S (2001). Prewriting and handwriting skills. In J. Case-Smith (Ed.). *Occupational Therapy for Children* (4th ed.). St Louis, MO. Mosby.

Aram D (2005). Continuity in children's literacy achievements: a longitudinal perspective from kindergarten to school. In *First Language*, 25 (3): 259–289.

Arslan D & Ilgin H (2010). Teachers' and students' opinions about cursive handwriting. In *Inonu University Journal of the Faculty of Education (INUJFE)*, 11 (2): 69–92.

Asperger H (1944). Autistic psychopathy in children. Translated in U Frith (1991). *Autism and Asperger Syndrome*. Cambridge. Cambridge University Press.

Assaiante C, Barlaam F, Cignetti F & Vaugoyeau M (2014). Body schema building during childhood and adolescence: a neurosensory approach. In *Clinical Neurophysiology*, 44 (1): 3–12.

Bara F & Gentaz E (2011). Haptics in teaching handwriting: the role of perceptual and visuo-motor skills. In *Human Movement Science*, 30 (4): 745–759.

Bara F, Morin MF, Alamargot D & Bosse ML (2016). Learning different allographs through handwriting: the impact on letter knowledge and reading acquisition. In *Learning and Individual Differences*, 47: 88–94.

Barnett A, Henderson SE, Scheib B & Schultz J (2007). Detailed Assessment of Speed of Handwriting (DASH). London. Pearson.

Barnett A, Henderson SE, Scheib B & Schultz J (2010). Detailed Assessment of Speed of Handwriting 17+ (DASH). London. Pearson.

Bazyk S, Michaud P, Goodman G, Papp P, Hawkins E & Welch MA (2009). Integrating occupational therapy services in a kindergarten curriculum: a look at the outcomes. In *American Journal of Occupational Therapy*, 63: 160–171.

Bear DR, Invernizzi M, Templeton S & Johnston F (2008). Words their way: word study for phonics, vocabulary, and spelling instruction (4th ed.). Upper Saddle River, NJ. Pearson/Prentice Hall.

Beard R & Burrell A (2010). Writing attainment in 9–11 year olds: some differences between girls and boys in two genres. In *Language and Education*, 24 (6): 495–515.

Bebey J, Engelstad K & Zapletal A (2014). Evaluating the effects of grasp patterns and grip strength on handwriting skills. Department of Occupational Therapy, Presentations. Paper 15. http://jdc.jefferson.edu/otpresentations/15

Beery K & Buktenica N (1997). Developmental test for visual motor integration. New Jersey. Modern Curriculum Press.

Benbow M (1991). Loops and other groups: a kinesthetic writing system instructor's manual. Tucson. Therapy Skill Builders.

Berninger V (2008). Evidence-based written language instruction during early and middle childhood. In Morris R & Mather N (Eds.) *Evidence-based interventions for students with learning and behavioural challenges*. Mahwah, NJ. Lawrence Erlbaum.

Berninger V & Richards T (2012). The writing brain: coordinating sensory/motor, language, and cognitive systems in working memory architecture. In Berninger V (Ed.). *Past, present, and future contributions of cognitive writing research to cognitive psychology.* New York. Psychology Press/Taylor Francis Group.

Bhopti A & Brown T (2013). Examining the Wilbargers's deep pressure and proprioceptive technique for treating children with sensory defensiveness using a multiple single case study approach. In *Journal of Occupational Therapy, Schools, and Early Intervention*, 6 (2): 108–130.

Blank R, Smits-Engelsman B, Polatajko H & Wilson PH (2011). European Academy for Childhood Disability (EACD): recommendations on the definition, diagnosis and intervention of developmental co-ordination disorder (long version). In *Developmental Medicine and Child Neurology*, 54: 54–93.

Blazer C (2010). Should cursive handwriting still be taught in schools? Information Capsule. In *Research Services*. Miami-Dade County Public Schools. drs.dadeschools.net/InformationCapsules/IC0916.pdf

Bosga-Stork IM, Bosga J, Ellis JL & Meulenbroek RJ (2015). Developing interactions between language and motor skills in the first three years of formal handwriting education. In *British Journal of Education, Society & Behavioural Science*, 12 (1): 1–13.

Brennan A (2012). Mirror writing and hand dominance in children: a new perspective on motor and perceptual theories. In *The Yale Review of Undergraduate Research in Psychology*: 12–23.

Brown CG (2010). Improving fine motor skills in young children: an intervention study. In *Educational Psychology in Practice: Theory, Research and Practice in Educational Psychology*, 26 (3): 269–278.

Brown T & Link J (2015). The association between measures of visual perception, visual-motor integration, and in-hand manipulation skills of school-age children and their manuscript handwriting speed. In *British Journal of Occupational Therapy*. doi: 10.1177/0308022615600179.

Bryden PJ, Pryde KM & Roy EA (2000). A performance measure of the degree of hand preference. In *Brain and Cognition* (44): 402–414.

Bryner J (2010). Ambidextrous children may have more problems in school. www.livescience.com/8044-ambidextrous-children-problemsschool.html

Burridge S & Wright S (2011). A review of Write Dance in the Early Years, (2nd ed.). In *Language and Education*, 25 (2): 180–182.

Caeyenberghs K, Tsoupas J, Wilson PH & Smits-Engelsman BCM (2009). Motor imagery development in primary school children. In *Developmental Neuropsychology*, 34: 103–121.

Callcott D (2012). Retained primary reflexes in pre-primary-aged indigenous children: the effect on movement ability and school readiness. In *Australasian Journal of Early Childhood*, 37 (2): 132–140.

Cantin N, Ryan J & Polatajko HJ (2014). Impact of task difficulty and motor ability on visual-motor task performance of children with and without developmental co-ordination disorder. In *Human Movement Science*, 34: 217–232.

Carlson AG, Rowe E & Curby TW (2013). Disentangling fine motor skills' relations to academic achievement: the relative contributions of visual-spatial integration and visual-motor co-ordination. In *The Journal of Genetic Psychology: Research and Theory on Human Development*, 174 (5): 513–533.

Celletti C, Castori M, Galli M, Rigoldi C, Grammatico P, Albertini G & Camerota F (2011). Evaluation of balance and improvement of proprioception by repetitive muscle vibration in a 15-year-old girl with joint hypermobility syndrome. In *Arthritis Care Research* (63): 775–779.

Chang SH & Yu NY (2010). Characterisation of motor control in handwriting difficulties in children with or without developmental co-ordination disorder. In *Developmental Medicine & Child Neurology*, 52: 244–250.

Cho ML, Kim DJ & Yang Y (2015). Effects of visual perceptual intervention on visual-motor integration and activities of daily living performance of children with cerebral palsy. In *Journal of Physical Therapy Science:* 27 (2): 411–413.

Clearfield MW (2004). The role of crawling and walking experience in infant spatial memory. In *Journal of Experimental Child Psychology*, 89: 214–241.

Coleman R, Piek JP & Livesey DJ (2001). A longitudinal study of motor ability and kinaesthetic acuity in young children at risk of developmental co-ordination disorder. In *Human Movement Science*, 20 (1–2): 95–110.

Connelly V, Gee D, & Walsh E (2007). A comparison of keyboarded and handwritten compositions and the relationship with transcription speed. In *British Journal of Educational Psychology*, 77 (2): 479–492.

Copley JA & Ziviani J (2010). Kinaesthetic Sensitivity and Handwriting Ability in Grade One Children. In *Australian Occupational Therapy Journal*, 37 (1): 39–43.

Cornhill H & Case-Smith J (1996). Factors that relate to good and poor handwriting. In *American Journal of Occupational Therapy*, 50: 732–739.

Cubelli R & Salla SD (2009). Mirror writing in pre-school children: a pilot study. In *Cognitive Processing*, 10: 101–104.

Danna J & Velay JL (2015). Basic and supplementary sensory feedback in handwriting. In *Frontiers in Psychology*, 6: 169.

De Beer M (2015). Crossing the midline of the body… how does it work? Johannesberg. Mind Moves Institution.

Dehaene S (2011). The massive impact of literacy on the brain and its consequences for education. In *Human Neuroplasticity and Education*. Pontifical Academy of Sciences, Scripta Varia 17, 201. www.pas.va/content/dam/accademia/pdf/sv117/sv117-dehaene.pdf

De Jager M (2006). Mind moves – remove the barriers to learning. Johannesburg. The ConneXion.

Dennis JL & Swinth Y (2001). Pencil grasp and children's handwriting legibility during different length writing tasks. In *American Journal of Occupational Therapy*, 55 (2): 175–183.

Denton P, Cope S & Moser C (2006). The effects of

sensorimotor-based intervention versus therapeutic practice on improving handwriting performance in 6- to 11-year-olds. In *American Journal of Occupational Therapy*, 60 (1): 16–27.

De Oliveira RF & Wann JP (2012). Driving skills of young adults with developmental co-ordination disorder: maintaining control and avoiding hazards. In *Human Movement Science*, 31 (3): 721–729.

Desorbay T (2013). A neuro-developmental approach to specific learning difficulties. In *International Journal of Nutrition, Pharmacology and Neurological Diseases*, 3 (1): 1–2.

De Vrie L, van Hartingsveldt MJ, Cup EHC, Nijhuis-van der Sanden MWG & De Groot IJM (2015). Evaluating fine motor co-ordination in children who are not ready for handwriting: which test should we take? In *Occupational Therapy International*, 22: 61–70.

Dinehart LH (2015). Handwriting in early childhood education: current research and future implications. In *Journal of Early Childhood Literacy*, 15 (1): 97–118.

Dockrell JE, Marshall CR & Wyse D (2016). Teachers' reported practices for teaching writing in England. In *Reading and Writing*, 29 (3): 409–434.

Donica DK, Goins A & Wagner K (2013). Effectiveness of Handwriting Readiness programs on postural control and letter and number formation in Head Start Classrooms. In *Journal of Occupational Therapy, Schools and Early Intervention*, 6 (2): 81–93.

Duiser IHF, van der Kamp J, Ledebt A & Savelsbergh GJP (2014). Relationship between the quality of children's handwriting and the Beery Buktenica developmental test of visuomotor integration after one year of writing tuition. In *Australian Occupational Therapy Journal*, 61: 76–82.

Ehrlich SB, Levine SC & Goldin-Meadow S (2006). The importance of gesture in children's spatial reasoning. In *Developmental Psychology*, 42 (6): 1259–1268.

Erhardt RP (2012). *Hand preference; theory, assessment and implications for function*. Maplewood USA. Erhardt Development Products.

Evans CL (2014). Does the use of educational technology and multi-modal learning experiences assist children in the development of early letter formation and handwriting skills, especially those with cross lateral preference? DEdPsy Thesis, Cardiff University. http://orca.cf.ac.uk/58614/

Exner C (1989). Development of hand functions. In Pratt PN & Allen AS (Eds.). *Occupational Therapy for Children*. St. Louis, MO. Mosby.

Exner C (1997). Clinical interpretation of in hand manipulation in young children: translation of movements. In *American Journal of Occupational Therapy*, 51: 729–732.

Exner C (2005). Development of hand skills. In J. Case-Smith (Ed.). *Occupational therapy for children* (5th ed.). St. Louis, MO. Mosby.

Falk TH, Tam C, Schwellnus H & Chau T (2010). Grip force variability and its effects on children's handwriting legibility, form, and strokes. In *Journal of Biomechanical Engineering*, 132 (11). 114504. http://dx.doi.org/10.1115/1.4002611

Feder KP & Majnemer A (2007). Handwriting development, competency, and intervention. In *Developmental Medicine and Child Neurology*, 49: 312–317.

Ferguson GD, Wilson PH & Smits-Engelsman BCM (2015). The influence of task paradigm on motor imagery ability in children with developmental co-ordination disorder. In *Human Movement Science*, 44: 81–90.

Fischer JP (2010). Capital letters mirror writing in children: a new hypothesis to unlock the mystery. In *Enfance*, 62: 371–386.

Fischer JP (2011). Mirror writing of digits and (capital) letters in the typically developing child. In *Cortex*, 47: 759–762.

Fischer JP & Koch AM (2016). Mirror writing in 5- to 6-year-old children: the preferred hand is not the explanation. In *Laterality: Asymmetries of Body, Brain and Cognition*, 21 (1): 34–49.

Fischer JP & Tazouti Y (2012). Unravelling the mystery of mirror writing in typically developing children. In *Journal of Educational Psychology*, 104 (1): 193–205.

Gardner MF (1998). Test of Handwriting Skills Revised (THS-R). Los Angeles, CA. Western Psychological Services.

Gerde HK, Foster TD & Skibbe LE (2014). Beyond the pencil: expanding the occupational therapist's role in helping young children to develop writing skills. In *The Open Journal of Occupational Therapy*, 2 (1): Article 5. doi.org/10.15453/2168-6408.1070

Gierach J (2009). Assessing Students' Needs for Assistive Technology (ASNAT): a resource manual for school district teams (5th ed.). Wisconsin Assistive Technology Initiative (WATI). www.wati.org/content/supports/free/pdf/Ch1-ATAssessment.pdf

Goddard Blythe S (2005). Releasing educational potential through movement: a summary of individual studies carried out using the INPP test battery and developmental exercise programme for use in schools with children with special needs. In *Child Care in Practice*, 11 (4): 415–432.

Goddard Blythe S (2009). *Attention, Balance and Co-ordinaton: the ABC of learning success*. Chichester. Wiley-Blackwell.

Gonçalves MA & Arezes PM (2012). Ergonomic design of classroom furniture for elementary schools. In Ahram TZ & Karowski W (Eds.). *Advances in Physical Ergonomics and Safety*. CRC Press.

Graham S (2010). Want to improve children's writing? Don't neglect their handwriting. In *American Educator*, 33 (4): 20–40.

Graham S, MacArthur CA & Fitzgerald J (Eds.) (2013). Best practices in writing instruction (2nd ed.). New York. Guilford Press.

Green CS & Bavelier D (2006). Effect of action video games on the spatial distribution of visuospatial attention. In *Journal of Experimental Psychology: Human Perception and Performance*, 32 (6): 1465–1478.

Green D, Chambers ME & Sugden DA (2008). Does subtype

of developmental co-ordination disorder count: is there a differential effect on outcome following intervention? In *Human Movement Science*, 27: 363–82.

Green T (2014). National Handwriting Day: 20 quotes about the power of writing. IBT Times. http://www.ibtimes.com/national-handwriting-day-20-quotes-about-power-writing-1546305 01/23/14

Gruber T, Meixner B, Prosser J & Sick B (2012). Handedness tests for preschool children: a novel approach based on graphics tablets and support vector machines. In *Applied Soft Computing*, 12 (4): 1390–1398.

Haan M (2015). Stability balls and handwriting proficiency in a kindergarten classroom. Master of Education Program Theses. Paper 86. http://digitalcollections.dordt.edu/med_theses/86

Hammond J, Jones V, Hill E, Green D & Male I (2014). An investigation of the impact of regular use of the Wii Fit to improve motor and psychosocial outcomes in children with movement difficulties: a pilot study. In *Child Care Health Development*, 40 (2): 165–175.

Hape K, Flood N, McArthur K, Sidara C, Stephens C & Welsh K (2014). A pilot study of the effectiveness of the Handwriting Without Tears® curriculum in first grade. In *Journal of Occupational Therapy, Schools, & Early Intervention*, 7: 3–4.

Hauck JA & Dewey D (2001). Hand preference and motor functioning in children with autism. In *Journal of Autism and Developmental Disorders*, 31 (3): 265–277.

Hepp-Reymond MC, Chakarov V, Schulte-Mönting J, Huethe F & Kristeva R (2009). Role of proprioception and vision in handwriting. In *Brain Research Bulletin*, 79 (6): 365–70.

Hoy MP, Egan MY & Feder K (2010). A systematic review of interventions to improve handwriting. In *Canadian Journal of Occupational Therapy*, 78: 13–25.

James KH (2010). Sensorimotor experience leads to changes in visual processing in the developing brain. In *Developmental Science*, 13: 279–288.

James KH & Atwood T (2009). The role of sensorimotor learning in the perception of like-letter forms: tracking the causes of neural specialisation for letters. In *Cognitive Neuropsychology*, 26 (1): 91–100.

James KH & Engelhardt L (2012). The effects of handwriting experience on functional brain development in pre-literate children. In *Trends in Neuroscience and Education*, 1 (1): 32–42.

James KH & Gauthier I (2006). Letter processing automatically recruits a sensory-motor brain network. In *Neuropsychologia*, 44: 2937–2949.

Jelsma D, Geuze RH, Mombarg R & Smits-Engelsman BC (2014). The impact of Wii Fit intervention on dynamic balance control in children with probable developmental co-ordination disorder and balance problems. In *Human Movement Science*, 33: 404–418.

Jenkins S (2015). We are slaves to the printed word, but only handwriting conveys real beauty. The Guardian. 20 August 2015. http://www.theguardian.com/commentisfree/2015/aug/20/printed-word-handwriting-meaning-calligraphy

Jongmans M, Linthorst-Bakker E, Westenberg Y & Smits-Engelsman B (2003). Use of a task-oriented self-instruction method to support children in primary school with poor handwriting quality and speed. In *Human Movement Science*, 22: 549–566.

Jordan-Black JA (2005). The effects of the Primary Movement programme on the academic performance of children attending ordinary primary school. In *Journal of Research in Special Educational Needs*, 5: 101–111.

Kaiser ML, Albaret JM & Doudin PA (2009). Relationship between visual-motor integration, eye-hand co-ordination, and quality of handwriting. In *Journal of Occupational Therapy, Schools, & Early Intervention*, 2: 87–95.

Kane K & Bell A (2009). A Core stability group program for children with Developmental Coordination Disorder: 3 clinical case reports. In *Paediatric Physical Therapy*, 21 (4): 375–382.

Kao Henry SR (1979). Handwriting Ergonomics. In *Visible Language*, 13 (3): 331–339.

Kavak ST & Bumin G (2009). The effects of pencil grip posture and different desk designs on handwriting performance in children with hemiplegic cerebral palsy. In *Jornel de Pediatria*, 85 (4): 346–352.

Lahav O, Apterb A & Ratzonc NZ (2013). Psychological adjustment and levels of self-esteem in children with visual-motor integration difficulties influences the results of a randomised intervention trial. In *Research in Developmental Disabilities*, 34 (1): 56–64.

Laufer L (1991). Callirobics. Charlottesville, VA. Callirobics Company.

Lee O (2014). Formal handwriting assessment for children with writing difficulties. In *Advanced Science and Technology Letters*, 59: 109–112.

Lifshitz N & Har-Zvi S (2015). A comparison between students who receive and who do not receive a writing readiness interventions on handwriting quality, speed and positive reactions. In *Early Childhood Education Journal*, 43 (1): 47–55.

Lindell AK & Hudry K (2013). Atypicalities in cortical structure, handedness and functional lateralisation for language in autism spectrum disorders. In *Neuropsychology Review*, 23 (3): 257–270.

Lombard A (2007). *Sensory integration – why it matters more than IQ and EQ*. Welgemoed. Metz Press.

Longcamp M, Bouchard C, Gilhodes JC, Anton JL, Roth M & Nazarian B (2008). Learning through hand- or typewriting influences visual recognition of new graphic shapes: behavioural and functional imaging evidence. In *Journal of Cognitive Neuroscience*, 20: 802–815.

Longcamp M, Boucard C, Gilhodes JC & Velay JL (2006). Remembering the orientation of newly learned characters depends on the associated writing knowledge: a comparison between handwriting and typing. In *Human Movement Science*, 25 (4–5): 646–656.

Longcamp M, Zerbato-Poudou MT & Velay JL (2005). The influence of writing practice on letter recognition in preschool children: a comparison between handwriting and typing. In *Acta Psychologica*, 119 (1): 67–79.

Lust CA & Donica DK (2011). Effectiveness of a Handwriting Readiness Program in Head Start: a two-group control trial. In *American Journal of Occupational Therapy*, 65 (5): 560–568.

Mackay N, McCluskey A & Mayes R (2010). The log handwriting program improved children's writing legibility: a pre-test–post-test study. In *American Journal of Occupational Therapy*, 64: 30–36.

Maldarelli JE, Kahrs BA, Hunt SC & Lockman JJ (2015). Development of early handwriting: visual-motor control during letter copying. In *Developmental Psychology*, 51 (7): 879–888.

Mangen A & Velay JL (2010). Digitising literacy: reflections on the haptics of writing. In Mehrdad HZ (Ed.). *Advances in Haptics*. InTech. www.intechopen.com/books/advances-in-haptics/digitizing-literacy-reflections-on-the-haptics-of-writing

Markoulakis R, Scharoun SM, Bryden J & Fletcher PC (2012). An examination of handedness and footedness in children with high functioning autism and Asperger syndrome. In *Journal of Autism and Developmental Disorders*, 42 (10): 2192–2201.

Marmoth E (2013). The relationship between brain dominance, body laterality and literacy skills in Grade 2 learners in a school in KZN. http://hdl.handle.net/10394/9174

McCarney D, Peters L, Jackson S, Thomas M & Kirby A (2011). Does poor handwriting conceal literacy potential in primary school children. In *International Journal of Disability, Development and Education*, 60 (2): 105–118.

McPhillips M & Jordan-Black JA (2007). Primary reflex persistence in children with reading difficulties (dyslexia): a cross-sectional study. In *Neuropsychologia*, 45: 748–754.

McPhillips M & Sheehy N (2004). Prevalence of persistent primary reflexes and motor problems in children with reading difficulties. In *Dyslexia*, 10 (4): 316–338.

Medimorec S & Risko EF (2016). Effects of disfluency in writing. In *British Journal of Psychology*. doi: 10.1111/bjop.12177

Medwell J & Wray D (2007). Handwriting: what do we know and what do we need to know? In *Literacy*, 4: 10–15.

Menz S, Hatten K & Grant-Beuttler M (2013). Strength training for a child with suspected Developmental Coordination Disorder. In *Paediatric Physical Therapy*, 25 (2): 214–223.

Michell D & Wood N (1999). An investigation of midline crossing in three-year-old children. In Physiotherapy, 85: 607–615.

Milone M (2007). Test of Handwriting Skills, Revised (THS-R). WPS Publisher.

Mombarg R, Jelsma D & Hartman E (2013). Effect of Wii-intervention on balance of children with poor motor performance. In *Research in Developmental Disabilities*, 34 (9): 2996–3003.

Mueller PA & Oppenheimer DM (2014). The pen is mightier than the keyboard: advantages of longhand over laptop note-taking. In *Psychological Science*, 25 (6): 1159–1168.

Nelson RA & Palmer SE (2007). Familiar shapes attract attention in figure-ground displays. In *Perception & Psychophysics*, 69 (3): 382–392.

Nistler R & Maiers A (2000). Stopping the silence: hearing parents' voices in an urban first-grade family literacy program. In *The Reading Teacher*, 53 (8): 670–680.

Ohl AM, Graze H, Weber K, Kenny S, Salvatore C & Wagreich S (2013). Effectiveness of a 10-Week Tier 1 response to intervention program in improving fine motor and visual–motor skills in general education kindergarten students. In *American Journal of Occupational Therapy*, 67: 507–514.

Olsen JZ (2001). Handwriting without tears® (8th ed.). Potomac.

Owen AJ (2009). Teachers' perceptions on the effectiveness of Write Dance as a method of improving handwriting skills. https://repository.cardiffmet.ac.uk/dspace/handle/10369/5075

Overvelde A & Hulstijn W (2011). Handwriting development in Grade 2 and Grade 3 primary school children with normal, at risk or dysgraphic characteristics. In *Research in Developmental Disabilities*, 3: 540–548.

Palmer S, Bailey S, Barker L, Barney L & Elliott A (2014). The effectiveness of therapeutic exercise for joint hypermobility syndrome: a systematic review. In *Physiotherapy*, 100 (3): 220–227.

Parush S, Bar-Effrat Hirsch I, Yinon M & Weintraub N (2009). Effectiveness of sensorimotor and task-oriented handwriting intervention in elementary school-aged students with handwriting difficulties. In *Participation and Health*, 29 (3): 125–134.

Parush S, Levanon-Erez N & Weintraub N (1998). Ergonomic factors influencing handwriting performance. In *Work*, 11: 295–305.

Perfetti CA & Tan LH (2013). Write to read: the brain's universal reading and writing network. In *Trends in Cognitive Sciences*, 17 (2): 56–57.

Peverly ST, Garner JK & Vekaria PC (2014). Both handwriting speed and selective attention are important to lecture note-taking. In *Reading and Writing*, 27 (1): 1–30.

Phelps J, Stempel L & Speck G (1984). Children's Handwriting Evaluation Scale. Texas. CHES.

Philip BA & Frey SH (2014). Compensatory changes accompanying chronic forced use of the non-dominant hand by unilateral amputees. In *The Journal of Neuroscience*, 34 (10): 3622–3631.

Pica R (2011). Should we teach handwriting in the digital age? Huffington Post. 19 October 2011.

Pinheiro RC, Martinez CMS & Fontaine AMJ (2014). Visual motor integration and overall development of pre-term and at-term children at the beginning of schooling. In *Journal of Human Growth and Development*, 24 (2): 181–187.

Pont K, Wallen M & Bundy A (2008). Reliability and validity of the test of in-hand manipulation in children ages 5 to 6 years. In *American Journal of Occupational Therapy*, 62 (4): 384–392.

Pont K, Wallen M & Bundy A (2009). Conceptualising

a modified system for classification of in-hand manipulation. In *Australian Occupational Therapy Journal*, 56: 2–15.

Pontart V, Bidet-Ildei C, Lambert E, Morisset P, Flouret L & Alamargot D (2013). Influence of handwriting skills during spelling in primary and lower secondary grades. In *Frontiers in Psychology*, 4: 818.

Poon KW, Li-Tsang CWP, Weiss TPL & Rosenblum S (2010). The effect of a computerised visual perception and visual-motor integration training program on improving Chinese handwriting of children with handwriting difficulties. In *Research in Developmental Disabilities*, 31 (6): 1552–1560.

Priya V & Rekha K (2015). Effects of wrist weighing in reducing upper limb tremors in patients with cerebellar lesions. In *International Journal of Physiotherapy and Research*, 3 (4): 1138–1141.

Proske U & Gandevia (2012). The proprioceptive senses: their roles in signaling body shape, body position and movement, and muscle force. In *Physiological Reviews*, 92 (4): 1651–1697.

Purcell-Gates V, Duke NK & Martineau JA (2007). Learning to read and write genre specific text: Roles of authentic experience and explicit teaching. In *Reading Research Quarterly*, 42 (1): 8–45.

Rabin E & Gordon A (2004). Tactile feedback contributes to consistency of finger movements during typing. In *Experimental Brain Research*, 155 (3): 362–369.

Ratzon N, Lahav O, Cohen-Metzger Y, Efraim D & Bart O (2009). Comparing different short-term service delivery methods of visual-motor treatment for first grade students in mainstream schools. In *Research in Developmental Disabilities*, 30 (6): 1168–1176.

Reutzel DR (2015). Early literacy research: findings primary-grade teachers will want to know. In *The Reading Teacher*, 69 (1): 14–24.

Rodriguez A, Kaakinen M, Moilanen I, Taanila A, McGough JJ, Loo S, McGough & Järvelin MR (2010). Mixed handedness is linked to mental health problems in children and adolescents. In *Pediatrics*, 125 (2): 340–348.

Rosenblum S, Goldstand S & Parush S (2006). Relationships among biomechanical ergonomic factors, handwriting product quality, handwriting efficiency, and computerized handwriting process measures in children with and without handwriting difficulties. In *American Journal of Occupational Therapy*, 60 (1): 28–39.

Rosenblum S & Josman N (2003). The relationship between postural control and fine manual dexterity. In *Physical and Occupational Therapy in Pediatrics*, 23: 47–57.

Rosenblum S, Weiss P & Parush S (2004). Handwriting evaluation for developmental dysgraphia: process versus product. In Reading & Writing: An Interdisciplinary Journal, 17: 433–458.

Russell H (2014). Signing off: Finnish schools phase out handwriting classes. www.theguardian.com/world/2015/jul/31/finnish-schools-phase-out-handwriting-classes-keyboard-skills-finland

Rysstad AL & Pedersen AV (2015). Brief Report: Non-right-handedness within the Autism Spectrum Disorder. In *Journal of Autism and Developmental Disorders*, 46 (3): 1110–1117.

Sajedi F & Barati H (2014). The effect of perceptual motor training on motor skills of preschool children. In *Iranian Rehabilitation Journal*, 12 (19): 14–17.

Sarma PSB (2008). Mixed handedness and achievement test scores of middle school boys. In *Perceptual and Motor Skills*, 107 (2): 497–506.

Scharoun SM & Bryden PJ (2014). Hand preference, performance abilities, and hand selection in children. In *Frontiers in Psychology*, 5 (82): 1–15.

Schott GD (2007). Mirror writing: neurological reflections on an unusual phenomenon. In *Journal of Neurology, Neurosurgery and Psychiatry*, 78 (1): 5–13.

Schwellnus H, Carnahan H, Kushki A, Polatajko H, Missiuna C & Chau T (2013). Writing forces associated with four pencil grasp patterns in Grade 4 children. In *American Journal of Occupational Therapy*, 67 (2): 218–227.

Smith KT (2013). Crossing the midline and its effect on handwriting structure and writing responses. Doctoral dissertation, St Mary's College of California.

Smith-Zuzovsky N & Exner CE (2004). The effect of seated position quality on typical 6- and 7-year-old children's object manipulation skills. In *American Journal of Occupational Therapy*, 58: 380–388.

Smits-Engelsman BCM, Blank R, Van Der Kaay AC, Mosterd-Van Der Maijs R, Vlugt Van Den Brand E, Polatatajko HJ & Wilson PH (2013). Efficacy of interventions to improve motor performance in children with developmental co-ordination disorder: a combined systematic review and meta-analysis. In *Developmental Medicine & Child Neurology*, 55: 229–237.

Soechting JF & Flanders M (2008). Sensorimotor control of contact force. In *Current Opinions Neurobiology*, 18: 565–572.

Stainthorp R & Rauf N (2009). An investigation of the influence of the transcription skills of handwriting and spelling on the quality of text writing by girls and boys in Key Stage 2. In *Handwriting Today*, 8: 8–13.

Stanberry K & Raskind MH (2009). Reading Rockets. Rickitt Educational Media Ltd.

Stevenson NC & Just C (2014). In Early Education, why teach handwriting before keyboarding? In *Early Childhood Education Journal*, 42 (1): 49–56.

Sudsawad P, Trombly CA, Henderson A & Tickle-Degnen L (2002). Testing the effect of kinaesthetic training on handwriting performance in first-grade students. In *American Journal of Occupational Therapy*, 56: 26–33.

Sumner E, Connelly V & Barnett AL (2013). Children with dyslexia are slow writers because they pause more often and not because they are slow at handwriting execution. In *Reading and Writing*, 26 (6): 991–1008.

Tarnai SB (2012). Inhibition-treatment of retained STNR (Symmetrical Tonic Neck Reflex) with a combination of extra lesson and chirophonetics therapy. In *Journal of Physical Therapy*, 4 (2): 61–74.

Teodorescu I & Addy LM (1996). *Write from the Start*. Hyde. LDA.

Terebova NN & Bezrukikh (2009). Characteristics of the development of visual perception in five to seven year old children. In *Human Physiology*, 35 (6): 684–689.

Thornton A, Licari M, Reid S, Armstrong J, Fallows R & Elliott C (2016). Cognitive orientation to (daily) occupational performance intervention leads to improvements in impairments, activity and participation in children with developmental co-ordination disorder. In *Disability Rehabilitation*, 38 (10): 979–986.

Tran US, Stieger S & Voracek (2014). Evidence for general right, mixed, and left-sidedness in self-reported handedness, footedness, eyedness and earedness, and a primary footedness in a large sample latent variable analysis. In *Neuropsychologia*, 62: 220–232.

Uehara I (2013). Left-right and up-down mirror image confusion in 4-, 5- and 6-year-olds. In *Psychology 4 (10)*: 736–740.

Uttal DH, Miller DI & Newcombe NS (2013). Exploring and enhancing spatial thinking links to achievement in science, technology, engineering, and mathematics? In *Current Directions in Psychological Science*, 22 (5): 367–373.

Van Hoorn JF, Maathuis CG, Peters LH, Hadders-Algra M (2010). Handwriting, visuomotor integration, and neurological condition at school age. In *Developmental Medicine & Child Neurology*, 52: 941–947.

Vinter A & Chartrel E (2008). Visual and proprioceptive recognition of cursive letters in young children. In *Acta Psychologica*, 129 (1): 147–156.

Vishnu P & Rekha K (2015). Effects of wrist weighting in reducing upper limb tremors in patients with cerebellar lesions. In *International Journal of Physiotherapy Research*, 3 (4): 1138–1141.

Visser M, Franzsen D (2010). The association of an omitted crawling milestone with pencil grasp and control in five- and six-year-old children. In *South African Journal of Occupational Therapy*, 40 (2): 19–23.

Visser M, Nel M, de Vrie J, Klopper E, Olën K & van Coller J (2014). In-hand manipulation of children aged four- and five-years-old: translation, rotation and shift movements. In Bloemfontein. *South African Journal of Occupational Therapy*, 44 (2): 22–28.

Vukelich C & Christie J (2009). Building a foundation for preschool literacy: effective instruction for children's reading and writing development (2nd ed). Newark, DE. International Reading Association Inc.

Vuoksima E, Koskenvuo M, Rose R & Kaprio J (2009). Origin of handedness: a nationwide study of 30161 adults. In *Neuropsychologia*, 47 (5): 1294–1301.

Vygotsky L (1978). Interaction between learning and development. In Gauvain M & Cole M (Eds.). *Readings on the development of children*. New York. Scientific American Books.

Wehrann S, Chiu T, Reid D & Sinclair G (2006). Evaluation of occupational therapy school-based consultation service for students with fine motor difficulties. In *Canadian Journal of Occupational Therapy*, 73 (4): 225–235.

Wicki W, Hurschler Lichtsteiner S, Saxer Geiger A & Müller M (2014). Handwriting fluency in children: impact and correlates. In *Swiss Journal of Psychology*, 73 (2): 87–96.

Willis J (2011). The brain-based benefits of writing for math and science learning. In *Edutopia*. The George Lukas Educational Foundation. 11 July 2011. www.edutopia.org/blog/writing-executive-function-brain-research-judy-willis

Wilson PH, Thomas PR & Maruff P (2002). Motor imagery training ameliorates motor clumsiness in children. In *Journal of Child Neurology*, 17 (7): 491–8.

Wolf BJ. Teaching Handwriting. In Birsh JR (2011). *Multisensory teaching of basic language skills (3rd ed.)*. Baltimore. Paul H Brookes Inc.

Wollscheid S, Sjaastad J & Tømte C (2016). The impact of digital devices vs. pen/cil and paper on primary school students' writing skills – a research review. In *Computers & Education*, 95: 19–35.

Yancosek KE & Calderhead WJ (2012). Efficacy of Handwriting For Heroes, a novel hand dominance transfer intervention. In *Hand Therapy*, 12 (1): 15–24.

Yancosek KE, Gulick K & Sammons A (2015). Handwriting for Heroes: learn to write with your dominant hand in six weeks (3rd ed.). MI USA. Loving Healing Press.

Young RA, Rose RV & Nelson R (2015). Teaching Fluent handwriting remediates many reading-related learning disabilities. In *Creative Education*, 6: 1752–1759.

Zurcher M (2016). Partnering with parents in the writing classroom. In *The Reading Teacher*, 69 (4): 367–376.

NOTES